French Racing Blue

French Racing Blue

Drivers, Cars and Triumphs of French Motor Racing

David Venables

Ian Allan
PUBLISHING

David Venables

Karl Ludvigsen

David Venables—Author

Formerly the Official Solicitor, David Venables is the Assistant Editor of the Vintage Sports Car Club Bulletin and a regular contributor to *The Automobile*. He is the author of motor racing histories on 1930s *Voiturette* racing Napier, Bugatti and Alfa Romeo and also the *Official Centenary History of Brooklands*. He lives in Sussex and is a keen vintage motorist, driving a 1930 Aston Martin and a 1936 Fiat.

Karl Ludvigsen—Series Editor

In addition to his motor industry activities as an executive (with GM, Fiat and Ford) and head of a consulting company, Karl Ludvigsen has been active for over 50 years as an author and historian. As an author, co-author or editor he has some fifty books to his credit—all of them about cars and the motor industry, Karl's life-long passion.

Since 1997 Karl Ludvigsen has been drawing on the photographic resources of the Ludvigsen Library to write and illustrate books on the great racing drivers, including Stirling Moss, Jackie Stewart, Juan Manuel Fangio, Dan Gurney, Alberto Ascari, Bruce McLaren, and Emerson Fittipaldi.

His introduction to *At Speed*, a book of Jesse Alexander's racing photography, won the Ken W. Purdy Award for Excellence in Automotive Journalism. He has written three times about Mercedes-Benz, twice about its racing cars. His books on the latter subject have won the Montagu Trophy (once) and the Nicholas-Joseph Cugnot Award (twice), both recognising outstanding automotive historical writing. In 2001 he again received the Cugnot award from the Society of Automotive Historians for his book about the early years of the Volkswagen, *Battle for the Beetle*. In 2002 the Society gave him its highest accolade, Friend of Automotive History.

Resident in England since 1980, Karl Ludvigsen is respected as a close and knowledgeable observer of, and participant in, the world motor industry. On motor industry topics Karl has written books about high-performance engines, the Wankel rotary engine, the histories of American auto makers and the V12 Engine.

He is a former technical editor of *Sports Cars Illustrated* (1956-57), editor of *Car and Driver* (1960-1962) and east coast editor of *Motor Trend* (1970s). His articles have been published in America by *Road & Track* and *Automobile Quarterly*, among others, while in Europe he writes frequently for *The Automobile*. He is a columnist for *Hemmings Sports & Exotic Cars* and Just-Auto.com.

Ludvigsen Library

All this book's illustrations are from the collection of the Ludvigsen Library or have been sourced for the book by the Library. Much in demand from publishers, editors, authors, enthusiasts, restorers and collectors, the Library's holdings include some 150,000 original negatives and more than 50,000 original transparencies. Print and digital files include some 100,000 images in addition to those held in negative form for a total approaching half a million images.

Available in the Library are high-quality images of Formula and sports-car racing, works visits, car tests, motor shows, personalities and domestic transport. Included are celebrated collections from the work of Rodolfo Mailander, Stanley Rosenthall, Max Le Grand, Cyril Posthumus, John Dugdale, Edward Eves and Ove Nielsen, also including the photography of Karl Ludvigsen. Early prints and glass negatives portray racing and motoring throughout the 20th Century. The Library website is **www.ludvigsen.com**

Steven Cavalieri—Artist

Artwork highlighting the designs of ten historic racing cars in this volume of the Racing Colours series has been created expressly for this work by Steven Cavalieri. With a youthful ambition 'to be a racing driver and a car designer,' Cavalieri studied at California's Art Center College of Design. After two decades as a creative director for various companies Cavalieri 'decided it was time to try to get back to a career involving cars.' He did so as a widely published illustrator of motor cars for auto publications.

Cavalieri's work strongly manifests his enthusiasm for his subject and his practical knowledge of automotive anatomy. He brings his own research resources to every project. With his insightful renderings featured in such publications as *Corvette Magazine* and *Classic & Sports Car*, Steven Cavalieri has gained recognition as a preeminent practitioner in his field. His portfolio may be viewed at **www.stevencavalieri.com**

French Racing Blue © 2009

ISBN 978 1 7110 3369 6

Produced by Chevron Publishing Limited
(www.chevronpublishing.co.uk)
Concept: Robert Forsyth
Project Editors: Robert Forsyth/Chevron Publishing
and Karl Ludvigsen
Cover and book design: Mark Nelson
© Text: David Venables
© Colour profiles: Steven Cavalieri

Published by Ian Allan Publishing
an imprint of Ian Allan Publishing Ltd. Hersham, Surrey, KT12 4RG

Printed by Ian Allan Printing Ltd. Hersham, Surrey, KT12 4RG
Disclaimer: The marque names and logos reproduced in this publication are used for illustrative and descriptive purposes pursuant to fair use exemptions under copyright and trade mark laws. For the avoidance of doubt, this book is not endorsed by or otherwise associated with the manufacturers whose names and logos are reproduced in this book and no such connection should be inferred.

Visit the Ian Allan Publishing website at:
www.ianallanpublishing.com

Ian Allan
PUBLISHING

CONTENTS

FOREWORD

This book, one of an unique series from Ian Allan Publishing, was conceived to introduce the reader to the cars, circuits, companies and characters of one of the great motor-sporting nations. Soon after the first races of 1895 the issue of nationality loomed large in Europe, birthplace of motoring. In fact the first major international motor race, the Gordon Bennett Cup of 1900 to 1905, was contested not by companies but by trios of cars representing their nations. Every part of every car had to be manufactured in the respective countries.

By the 1920s cars from France, Germany, Great Britain, the United States, Italy and Austria were prominent in international motor sports, distinguished by their official national colours. With the rebirth of assertive nationalism in the 1930s their colours took on new significance as the flag-bearers of European nations took to the tracks to demonstrate their skills and superiority.

After World War Two their colours bespoke the nationality of racing cars until the late 1960s, when liveries were allowed to reflect sponsorship. Though this relaxation of constraints did produce fabulous-looking racing cars, some competitors continued to reflect their countries of construction in their choice of colours. Because national identities are blurred when French racing cars are made in Britain and German cars are produced in Switzerland—as they are in the 21st Century—the new paradigm can be seen to have its merits.

Introduced, explained and illustrated in these pages are the companies, engineers, executives and enthusiasts whose powerful competitive spirit and dauntless courage drove them to dominate in motor racing. It has been my pleasure to reveal the dramatic stories behind their successes and failures in the great classic endurance races and Grand Prix contests in which they dominated—or faced disaster. Motor racing, which has no equal in the ecstasy of victory and agony of defeat, comes vividly to life in this volume's colourful pages.

Karl Ludvigsen
Series Editor

MANUFACTURING SITES:

1. **PARIS**: Delahaye, Talbot, Gordini, Citroën, Mors

   PARIS (environs of Paris)

   COURBEVOIE: Delage

   EVRY: Renault

   ST. DENIS: Amilcar

   VÉLIZY-VILLACOUBLAY: Matra/Peugeot

   VIRY-CHÂTILLON: Renault

   PUTEAUX: Peugeot

   GENEVILLIERS: Chenard-Walcker

   ISSY-LES-MOULINEAUX: Voisin

   LEVALLOIS-PERRET: BNC

   COURBEVOIE: Lombard

   BILLANCOURT: Renault/Salmson

2. **MOLSHEIM**: Bugatti
3. **THORIGNY**: WM
4. **VICHY**: Ligier
5. **MAGNY-COURS**: Martini
6. **LUNÉVILLE**: Lorraine-Dietrich

EARLY OPEN ROAD RACES, LAND SPEED RECORDS, MAJOR CIRCUITS & HILL CLIMBS:

7. **ACHERES**: Land speed records
8. **AMIENS**
9. **ARPAJON**: Land speed records
10. **BORDEAUX**: Early open road races
11. **BOULOGNE**
12. **COMMINGES**
13. **CLERMONT-FERRAND**
14. **DIEPPE**
15. **DIJON**
16. **DOURDAN**
17. **LE MANS**
18. **LYON**
19. **MAGNY-COURS**
20. **MARSEILLES**
21. **MIRAMAS**
22. **MONACO**
23. **MONTLHÉRY**
24. **PAU**
25. **PAUL RICARD**
26. **REIMS**
27. **ROUEN**: Circuit and early open road races
28. **STRASBOURG**
29. **TOULOUSE**: Early open road races
30. **LA TURBIE**: Hill climbs
31. **MONT VENTOUX**: Hill climbs

French manufacturing sites of racing cars—past and present—early open road races, land speed records, major racing circuits and hill climbs used

CHAPTER I

The Beginnings: Brave Pioneers

Almost the first: the 1883 De Dion steam tricycle

FRANCE, the birthplace of motor racing, nurtured the sport during its early tentative years. Although the petrol internal-combustion engine first emerged in Germany, France was the nation where the motor car was encouraged and developed.

Before Benz and Daimler produced their first primitive engines, manufacturers in France were already building and even marketing steam-powered road vehicles. Young engineer Amédée Bollée, working in Le Mans, built a successful steam car, 'L'Obéissante', in 1871. This vehicle, which looked somewhat like a railway carriage, was followed by a much more advanced machine, 'La Mancelle', which had its steam engine under the bonnet in front of the driver and was driven by its rear wheels.

Meanwhile in 1881 a French aristocrat, Count Albert de Dion, had joined forces with an engineer, Georges Bouton. He encouraged the fitting of a Bouton steam engine into a vehicle built by Trépardoux et Cie at Puteaux in the suburbs of Paris. The De Dion, Bouton & Trépardoux steam vehicle went into limited production and was offered for sale.

Gottlieb Daimler in Germany began manufacturing petrol-fuelled engines. Though he intended these initially for industrial use, a licence to make the engines in France was negotiated by Emil Levassor, who with his partner René Panhard had been making gas engines and industrial machinery as Panhard & Levassor. The latter did a deal with bicycle manufacturer Armand Peugeot to supply engines for cars which Peugeot wanted to build.

The first Peugeots emerged in 1890 from a works at Valentigney south of Belfort in Eastern France and were soon followed by the first Panhard & Levassor as the partners realised the potential of the new market. Early Peugeot cars were beautifully engineered, in contrast to those offered by most other pioneer manufacturers.

The desire to compete is one of the major instincts in mankind. In 1887, realising this, M. Fossier, proprietor of the magazine *Vélocipède*, organised the first motoring competition over a short course on the outskirts of Paris.

This 1894 Peugeot was adjudged to have won the first motor race from Paris to Rouen.

Only one runner turned up, a steam car driven by Count de Dion, who duly completed the course. After that, although various manufacturers did publicise long-distance runs in France, there was a lull.

In 1894 Pierre Giffard of *Le Petit Journal* decided there was a need to bring the emerging motor car to the notice of a wider public. He announced that he would organise a race from Paris to Rouen in the summer of 1894. The response was remarkable, attracting 102 entries. After the date was postponed twice to give entrants more time for preparation, the race was run on 22 July 1894.

Eventually 21 cars came to the line. They were released on the road to Rouen covering a course of approximately 80 miles (126 km). Remarkably, 17 finished. The first car to arrive at Rouen after 6 hours and 48 minutes on the road was a steam-powered De Dion driven by the Count. This was followed three minutes later by a Peugeot driven by Lemaitre. Unfortunately for the Count he was disqualified as it was decreed that the De Dion needed a stoker to keep it going, as well as the driver, so the honour of winning the first motor race went to Peugeot. A tradition of cars falling foul of the regulations in motor racing has thrived ever since.

The success of the Paris-Rouen was followed in November 1894 by the formation of the Automobile Club de France (ACF). The new club immediately began organising a much more testing event. This was to run from Paris to Bordeaux and back to Paris. It began on 11 June 1895, the 22 starters facing a course of 732 miles (1,177 km). The winner, the Panhard & Levassor of Emile Levassor, took four days to return to Paris, having averaged 15 mph (24 km/h), and was rewarded with a prize of 12,600 francs. Koechlin, driver of the third-placed Peugeot, received the much bigger prize of 31,500 francs as his car had four seats. The winning car had a 1,206 cc vertical twin Phoenix engine which had been designed by Daimler in Germany.

More than 100 years later it is hard to appreciate the conditions faced by these pioneer racing drivers. They drove on roads which were often little more than rolled gravel. In dry summer weather dust obscured everything, especially the road ahead. They coped with primitive steering, minimal or almost non-existent brakes and their cars were unreliable, needing constant attention. The harsh

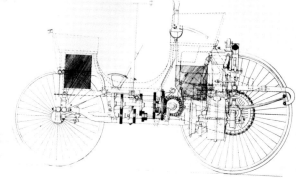

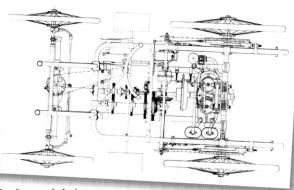

Drawings depict the 1894 Peugeot.

suspension and iron-shod or solid rubber-rimmed wheels gave both driver and passengers a relentless pounding. They faced horse-drawn traffic wholly unused to the motor car. Sometimes the inhabitants of the towns and villages through which they drove were hostile—often with good reason.

Of two races in the spring of 1896 the longer was from Bordeaux to Agen and back again, a distance of about 171 miles (275 km). It was won by a Peugeot. The ACF had grander ambitions and so organised a race from Paris to Marseilles and back to Paris. The original date clashed with a state visit to France by the Czar of Russia so it was rearranged for 24 September.

To weed out less capable vehicles, including motor tricycles, an eliminating race was held from Paris to Mantes and back again, about 64 miles (103 km), the weekend before the big race. The first five finishers qualified to go to Marseilles, of which four were the new De Dion tricycles. Georges Bouton had realised the limitations of steam and had designed and built his own petrol engine, eschewing the German-built and -licenced products.

The field comprised 24 petrol-fuelled cars, three steam cars and the five tricycles. They assembled by the Arc de Triomphe and went in single file to Versailles where they were released on their journey. The course to Marseilles was in four stages, on the second of which a violent storm swept across France. The roads collapsed and were blocked by fallen trees, causing many accidents. Charged by a bull, Bollée's car was too badly damaged to continue.

Eighteen cars left Dijon for the third stage with the leader Levassor in a Panhard, but he hit a dog near Orange and overturned. Though he only appeared shaken he suffered injuries which may have been a cause of his death about six months later when he collapsed at his drawing board. Fifteen cars reached Marseilles and, after a day's rest, turned round and started the trip back to Paris.

The appalling conditions of the outward journey and the operation of Darwin's theory of natural selection weeded out the less-fit cars so there were few drop-outs on the return to Paris. The 14 finishers reached the city on 4 October and received a rapturous reception. The race was a triumph for the Panhards which took first, second and fourth places. Splitting the Panhards in third place was a De Dion tricycle whose rider had pedalled most of the way from Marseilles to Paris.

The winning 2.4-litre Panhard, driven by Mayade, went to England a month later to take part in the London to Brighton Emancipation Run. It subsequently stayed in England and became the embryo from which the first British racing car, the Napier, evolved.

Surprisingly, after the success of the Paris-Marseilles-Paris race, there was subdued activity in 1897. A 149-mile (239-km) event from Marseilles to Nice was won by a De Dion while Panhards scooped the prizes in runs from Paris to Dieppe and to Trouville. It was significant, though, that one of the Panhards in the Trouville race had a sleeker and more aerodynamic body. Previously standard-bodied touring cars had been raced, but the specialised competition machine was beginning to emerge.

Another development was the almost universal adoption of the pneumatic tyre. The disadvantages of frequent punctures were wholly outweighed by the benefits of comfort and handling while tyre technology was improving rapidly.

After the relative lull in 1897 a flurry of activity followed. The 1898 season began in March with a two-day race from Marseilles to Nice. This was another Panhard success. The winning car, driven by Fernand Charron, attracted attention as it was painted white; until then cars had been finished in sombre colours. As almost every car which competed was of French manufacture, thoughts of national colours had not arisen, nor did manufacturers seem to have chosen distinctive colour schemes.

There was a setback on 1 May when a local race, the Course de Perigueux, was held in the Dordogne. This was a single circuit of a 90 mile (144 km) course. Soon after the start a Parisienne, a Benz built under licence in Paris, collided with an MLB. When the Parisienne overturned its mechanic was badly hurt. The Marquis de Montaignac, the

Panhard was victorious in the Paris-Marseille-Paris race in September of 1896.

driver of the tiller-steered MLB, looked round at the Parisenne and went off the road. The MLB overturned and the Marquis and his mechanic were both fatally injured. This was the first death in motor racing.

Two weeks after the Perigueux disaster a race was run from Paris to Bordeaux with an overnight stop at Tours. Organised by *Le Velo* newspaper and given the title of '*Criterium des Entraineurs*', it drew a modest field of nine starters who lined up for an innovation, a massed start. Despite the dangers of a narrow road, there was no mishap. Once again it was a Panhard win. Now with new four-cylinder 3.3-litre engines, the work of Arthur Krebs, who had taken over the design after Levassor's death, the three 'works' cars were painted red, white and blue. Victory went to the blue-painted car of De Knyff. The winner's average was 22 mph (35 km/h). Speeds were increasing.

The major race of the year, organised by the ACF, showed increasing ambition as the course ran from Paris to Amsterdam and then back to Paris. The total distance was 889 miles (1,430 km). This would be the first international race crossing national frontiers. There were three outward stages and three on the return.

The start was to be at Champigny, outside Paris, but the local *Préfet*—who abhorred motor cars—refused to issue the certificates necessary to drive on French roads. The drivers decided to start anyway, but the *Préfet* called out the army to close the course and mounted field guns on the route. The drivers, feeling there would be enough hazards en route without artillery fire, agreed that the start should be moved to Villiers outside the Préfet's Department so that the race could begin without bother.

Forty-eight cars started and 37 reached the end of the first stage. The pace was quick with Charron averaging 32 mph (51 km/h). The four-cylinder 2.4-litre Panhards had a major improvement, being fitted with wheel steering in place of the former tiller, and were again the fastest cars. Giradot was the leader at Amsterdam while Charron had been pushed down to third place by the Bollée of Giraud. The Bollées with pointed noses and tails were called 'torpedoes'.

The three-cornered battle for the lead continued on the return journey. Giradot started the last stage with a lead of nine minutes, but lost over half an hour with punctures and so Charron came home to the winner's reception at Versailles. The route of the final stage had been changed at the last minute to avoid the vengeful *Préfet* and his artillery ordnance.

After several minor races in November of 1898 a speed trial was organised by *La France Automobile* at Achères. The Count de Chasseloup Laubat brought out an electric-

powered Jeanteaud and set the fastest time over a flying kilometre at 39.3 mph (63.2 km/h) which constituted the first World Land Speed record.

Technical problems prevented another electric-powered driver, Paris-based Belgian Camille Jenatzy, from competing at Achères. He believed he had the faster car and so challenged the Count to a head-to-head match. They were already rivals. Both built cabs in Paris and had been competitors in the Paris Motor Cab Trials in 1898.

They met on 17 January 1899 when Jenatzy recorded 41.4 mph (66.6 km/h). The Count replied with 43.7 mph (70.3 km/h) and would have gone faster had his motor not burned out before the finish. Jenatzy tried again and pushed the record up to 50.0 mph (80.4 km/h) to which the Count

Jenatzy's Mors was the worse for wear after his accident in the 1899 Tour de France.

Shown by a replica was Jenatzy's electric-powered 'La Jamais Contente' in which he set a World Land Speed record of 65.75 mph (105.79 km/h) in 1899.

PARIS-ROUEN

The Paris-Rouen contest was the world's first recognised motor race. Organised and sponsored by the Paris newspaper 'Le Petit Journal', it was held on Sunday 22 July 1894. Some of its 102 entries were powered by such bizarre methods as 'weight of passengers' and 'system of levers'. The more outlandish modes of propulsion never left the drawing board or even the fevered imagination of the inventor. The entry was weeded out by a preliminary trial four days earlier, when the entrants had to show a modicum of efficiency by covering a course of about 30 miles (48 km). On the day of the race 21 cars arrived at the start in the Boulevard Maillot in Paris, all either petrol- or steam-powered. The first left Paris at 8:00 a.m. on the 80-mile (130-km) journey, followed by the rest at 30-second intervals. There was a compulsory lunch stop at Mantes. For many of the runners it was little more than a social outing, though there was fierce competition among the front runners.

The steam-powered De Dion led the way on a route lined with spectators, who cheered and threw flowers at the competitors. There were problems with poor road surfaces. The De Dion took a wrong turning, ending in a potato field. However, back on the road it was the first to arrive at the Champ de Mars in Rouen at about 5:40 p.m. Only four cars failed to finish the course.

Although the De Dion, driven by Count De Dion, finished with a lead of three and a half minutes over the Peugeot of

The steam-powered De Dion was the first finisher in the 1894 Paris-Rouen race.

Lemaitre, the Count was denied the first prize. It was decreed that his machine was not solely controlled by the driver, as it needed the attention of a stoker mechanic. The De Dion was demoted to second, the first prize of FFr5,000 going to the Peugeot. Thus the first motor race was won by a Peugeot, a name that would still be prominent in motor racing over a century later.

riposted with a run on 4 April of 57.6 mph (92.6 km/h). Jenatzy went away and built a new cigar-shaped car, 'La Jamais Contente'. Painted blue, this ran at Achères on 29 April and recorded 65.75 mph (105.79 km/h). The Count had no answer to Jenatzy's World record, which would stand for three years.

The first major race of 1899 was the Paris-Bordeaux, now becoming a regular fixture. It was run as a single stage of 351 miles (563 km) with another immensely hazardous mass start. Fortunately there was only one collision, in which a mechanic was hurt. Panhard victories were coming with almost monotonous regularity. At the finish in Bordeaux the marque took the first five places, led home by the white car of Charron.

The next event on the calendar was the even more ambitious Tour de France. Starting in Paris the route ran to Nancy, Aix-les-Bains, Vichy, Perigueux, Nantes and Cabourg before returning to Paris, a distance of 1,350 miles (2,172 km). Engines were getting bigger with the Panhard team now having units of 4,398 cc. Despite strong opposition from a team of four-cylinder 4,224 cc Mors led by Jenatzy and 'Levegh'—whose name was Alfred Velghe—the Panhards triumphed once again, taking the first four

places, with De Knyff the winner. Mors had begun as an electrical manufacturer in Paris in the mid-19th Century, but in 1898 started producing cars, designed by Richard Brasier—soon to make cars himself.

The Mors had their revenge, taking first and second places in the Paris-St.Malo at the end of July. Then came a remarkable race in September, the Paris-Ostend. From its mass start Giradot with his Panhard and 'Levegh' in a Mors duelled all the way at speeds up to 60 mph (95 km/h). They crossed the finishing line on Ostend race course so closely that it was adjudged a dead heat. Their average was 32.5 mph (52.2 km/h).

Two weeks later Giradot won the Paris-Boulogne by 1 minute 36 seconds from 'Levegh', who finished the season with a win in the Bordeaux-Biarritz on 1 October. After several seasons of dominance Panhard was finally being challenged. In five years racing had grown from a demanding test of reliability to fierce wheel-to-wheel battles at high speeds, almost always amid thick clouds of dust. It was about to change.

Serpollet set a new World record in his steam car at the Nice Speed week in 1902, recording 75.06 mph (120.77 km/h).

The British driver Charles Jarrott piloted this 40 hp Panhard in the 1901 Paris-Berlin race.

13

CHAPTER 2

The Open Road:
Mors, Renault and Panhard Battle for Supremacy

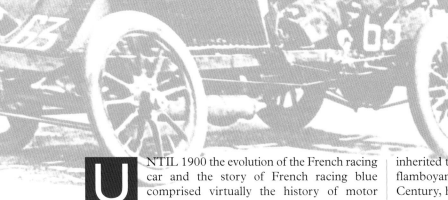

The Renault in which Marcel Renault won the 1902 Paris-Vienna race came to life again in a replica.

UNTIL 1900 the evolution of the French racing car and the story of French racing blue comprised virtually the history of motor racing. The influence of one man was to bring great change. James Gordon Bennett, Jr. was born in 1841. His father had founded the *New York Herald*. James Jr., who inherited the newspaper and his father's wealth, enjoyed a flamboyant life. Living in Paris at the end of the 19th Century, he was interested in the development of the car and in 1899 offered a trophy to the ACF. This was to be raced for annually by teams of three cars selected by the national automobile clubs. It was a stipulation that every component of the competing cars had to be made in the country which they were representing. The winning country would stage the following year's race.

The French motor racing community was not over-impressed by the Gordon Bennett proposals. The 1900 season began with the usual open-road events, then there was a set-back in April. During the Paris-Roubaix race for motor tricycles one machine went off the road and struck the wife of the *Préfet* of the Seine-Oise Department, breaking her leg. The outcome was an immediate ban imposed by the *Préfet* on all racing in his Department, followed by a similar edict from the Minister of the Interior affecting all France. The Minister reserved the right to sanction individual races. The ACF handled the matter tactfully. A month later the Bordeaux-Perigueux race was approved and found the Mors of 'Levegh' beating the Panhards again.

Only three cars could represent France in the first Gordon Bennett race. The ACF chose the 24 HP 5.3-litre

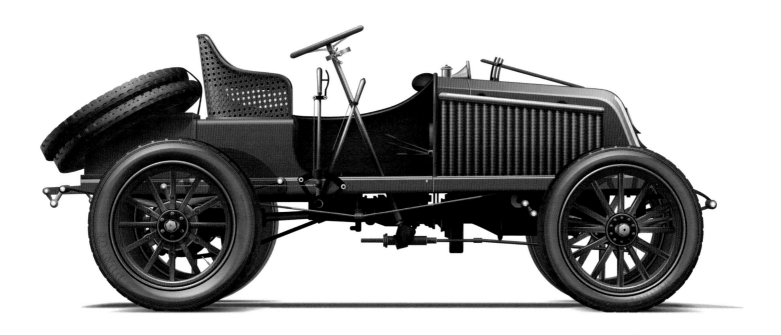

1902 Type K Renault

The 3.8-litre Type K Renault caused a sensation when it won the 1902 Paris–Vienna race. Driven by Marcel Renault and running in the Light Car class, it defeated the large-capacity cars and set a new standard.

The Chevalier de Knyff posed in his Panhard before the start of the 1903 Paris-Madrid race.

The outward leg was only a day, but the return to Paris was over two days with a stop at Limoges. The total distance was 837 miles (1,346 km). The race began at 3:30 a.m., but the slower cars were still running towards Toulouse when night fell.

'Levegh' in a Mors won the opening stage but was plagued with tyre problems on the two return stages to Paris. Voight, who was driving the Gordon-Bennett winning Panhard, was the fastest on these stages but 'Levegh' had built up such a margin on the opening stage that he was the winner. He completed the course at an average of 40.2 mph (64.7 km/h). Engines were getting bigger and the Mors had a capacity of 7.3 litres.

A *Voiturette* class for smaller cars weighing less than 400 kg was becoming popular. A new manufacturer, Renault, had entered a single-cylinder De Dion-engined 498 cc car for this class in the Paris-Toulouse-Paris. The red-painted machine vibrated its way to Paris as the winner, driven by Louis Renault.

The French manufacturers had a wake-up call in March 1901 when a Mercedes won the 243-mile (390-km) Nice-Salon-Nice race. The ACF had realised that the Gordon Bennett had insufficient appeal as a race standing alone, so it was included as a concurrent event with the Paris-Bordeaux contest in May 1901. The claim of 'Levegh' could not be denied. He was in the Gordon Bennett team with a new Mors fitted with a 10-litre engine. His team mates were Charron and Giradot with 40 HP 7.4-litre Panhards. The Mercedes team was withdrawn and the only foreign challenge was Edge's Napier.

Charron soon fell by the wayside with valve problems and Levegh also dropped out, but fortunately for French pride Giradot was able to finish, albeit in seventh place in the Paris-Bordeaux field, but this retained the Gordon Bennett Trophy for France. In the main race Henri Fournier's Mors led home five Panhards. His race average was 53 mph (85 km/h). A 3.3-litre Panhard won the class for light cars weighing between 400 and 650 kg while Louis Renault carried off the *Voiturette* class again with a Type E using a 1,234 cc De Dion single-cylinder engine.

The Paris-Bordeaux was a preliminary for the major race of the year and the most ambitious yet. The Paris-Berlin contest was held on 27, 28 and 29 June. The 687-mile (1,105-km) route ran through Reims, Aachen, Cologne, Düsseldorf and Hanover. With the runners in the light car and *Voiturette* classes there were 110 starters.

The first leg to Aachen was full of incident with crashes and accidents. Unfortunately a boy spectator was killed. Despite many punctures, Fournier was the leader, his Mors followed by the Panhards of de Knyff and Voight.

Panhards of de Knyff, Charron and Giradot. This caused a furious outcry, especially from the successful Mors drivers. 'Levegh' threatened to obtain a Belgian licence. It was recommended that the teams should race in distinctive national colours with blue allocated to the French team; so a magnificent tradition had begun.

The race was held on 14 June over a course from Suresnes to Versailles, Chartres, Orléans, Nevers and on to Lyon, a distance of 353 miles (567 km). Apart from the three Panhards there were only two other starters. Jenatzy, wearing his Belgian hat again, was in a Bolide and the American Winton was driving a car of his own manufacture. The race was won by Charron with Giradot second. The two Panhards were the only finishers. Charron had a narrow escape when he collided with a St. Bernard dog which jammed the steering and he went off the road, but was able to carry on unscathed.

With the distraction of the Gordon Bennett out of the way, French drivers returned to serious racing. Paris-Toulouse-Paris was run between 25 and 28 July.

The second day began in mist but ended in hot sun with the inevitable dust. The lead was exchanged between Fournier and his Panhard rivals, but he reached Hanover in first place.

On the final stage to Berlin Henri Fournier led again and arrived at the Berlin trotting track to be acclaimed by a huge crowd as the winner, having averaged 44.1 mph (70.9 km/h). He was followed by the Panhards of Giradot and de Knyff. It was evident that Mors had displaced Panhard at the top of the French tree. In an amazing eighth place amongst the 47 finishers was the little Type E Renault driven by Louis Renault, who was showing indications of greatness to come.

The fatal accident to the spectating youth during the Paris-Berlin race had serious repercussions. In the autumn of 1901 a ministerial ban on racing over public roads in France was imposed. Despite this, the ACF was busy organising a race from Paris to Vienna which would include the 1902 Gordon Bennett competition. Realising that cars were becoming too big and too fast, a maximum weight limit of 1,000 kg was imposed.

With a burst of 'green' fervour which would have been applauded 100 years later, the French government lifted the racing ban for the Circuit du Nord in May 1902 but required all competitors to run on alcohol fuel as a boost for French agriculture. The cars followed a circuitous route from Paris to Arras thence back to Paris via Boulogne. Passing without major incident, the race was won by the 40 HP Panhard of Maurice Farman, who was later to achieve fame as an aircraft manufacturer. He was followed home by the similar car of the British driver Charles Jarrott. Panhard used the race as a try-out for a

A Pyrrhic victory: Fernand Gabriel's Mors was impounded after winning the stage to Bordeaux of the 1903 Paris-Madrid.

new 70 HP 13.6-litre car intended for the Paris-Vienna, which finished eighth.

The Paris-Vienna had three stages. The first ran from Paris to Belfort and thence to a neutralised zone running through Switzerland. The racing began again on the second stage from Bregenz to Salzburg and then from Salzburg to Vienna. It was a total of 615 miles (989 km) but the Gordon Bennett competitors only had to motor as far as Salzburg, a mere 430 miles (692 kms), the stipulated 500 km being taken up by the non-racing Swiss leg.

The ACF had an easier choice when picking its French team. 'Levegh' had retired from the sport. He had tuberculosis and would die the following year. Charron too had retired and had become a manufacturer, setting up a new company with Giradot and Voight, CGV. Giradot was chosen with a CGV. Fournier was an obvious choice with a new 60 HP 9.2-litre Mors and the third member was de Knyff with the new Panhard. Although the Gordon Bennett finished at Salzburg, the competitors were also in the Paris-Vienna and were expected to go the full distance for greater glory. The only other team entered for the Gordon Bennett

came from Britain with Selwyn Edge's Napier and two Wolseleys.

The Gordon Bennett was a French disaster. The Mors and CGV dropped out on the first stage before reaching Belfort and de Knyff stopped on the Arlberg Pass with a broken back axle, leaving Edge to take an unexpected win for Britain. In the Paris-Vienna there was a sensation. Until his axle broke, de Knyff had been leading, battling with the Panhards of Henri and Maurice Farman while all were being pushed by a Mercedes in the hands of Count Zborowski.

The huge crowd gathered at the Prater trotting track on the outskirts of Vienna was astounded when the first car to appear was the muddy and dust-coated red Renault of Marcel Renault. It was a tuned version of a new model, the 3.8-litre four-cylinder Type K. Renault had finished 13 minutes in front of Henri Farman, also taking the light-car class, while Zborowski was third.

The Belgians have been unfairly stereotyped as dull and unimaginative. In July of 1902 the AC de Belgique showed notably more creativity and foresight than their French

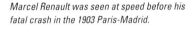

Marcel Renault was seen at speed before his fatal crash in the 1903 Paris-Madrid.

Marcel Renault crashed fatally in the truncated 1903 Paris-Madrid race.

PARIS-MADRID

Motor racing burgeoned in its early years, almost every race being held between cities over open roads. The performance of the cars increased rapidly and by 1903 the fastest were capable of over 90 mph (145 km/h). Race organisers vied to put on better and better races. The Automobile Club de France aimed to scoop the pool with the most ambitious race of all through much of France and Spain. Initially the French government opposed its plan but bowed to regal support from King Alfonso of Spain.

The epic race was held on 24 May 1903, running from Paris to Madrid via Bordeaux, where an overnight stop was scheduled. Entries totalled 192 cars. All the leading French manufacturers were represented and all the leading drivers took part. It has been estimated that over a million spectators watched the race. Along the course they crowded the roadside, standing in front of approaching cars and only stepping back at the last moment.

With the increased speed of the cars, the huge crowds and the poor road surfaces, the outcome was inevitable. In the many crashes five competitors—among them Marcel Renault—and three spectators were killed. Cars had grown in nine years from puttering novelties to thundering machines whose power had vastly outgrown the capabilities of the chassis and especially the tyres.

Reports of the carnage which reached Paris were exaggerated, triggering immediate calls for the 'Race to Death' to be stopped. When the cars reached Bordeaux the drivers were told the race was over. The cars were impounded, towed by horses to the railway station and returned to Paris by freight train. The race almost brought a ban on motor racing. From it however came racing on closed circuits with proper crowd protection. The sport as it is known today began to evolve.

counterparts. Instead of the usual frenetic town-to town dash over open roads, the ACB organised the Circuit des Ardennes which was—as its title indicates—a circuit race over six laps of a 53-mile (85-km) course in the Ardennes region. The road was partly closed. It was a victory for Briton Charles Jarrott with a 70 HP Panhard, defeating the Mors of Fernand Gabriel and the American William Vanderbilt, while Zborowski was fourth with a Mercedes.

The ACF felt the need to promote bigger and better races. After the success of its Paris-Vienna an even more ambitious plan was hatched for 1903: a race from Paris to Madrid. The French government indicated that it would not sanction the race, but when the ACF gained the support of King Alfonso of Spain all governmental opposition faded away. The first leg would run from Paris to Bordeaux over the well-used route.

This was a race that all the French manufacturers wanted to win, the greatest race yet. The weight limit had not reduced the size or power of the engines. The cars lined up at dawn outside Versailles on Sunday 24 May were the most powerful yet seen. The race had attracted huge publicity and it has been estimated that over a million spectators lined the route. The drivers found that the crowds pushed forward and blocked the road, only moving back as a car approached.

At the first control at Rambouillet, de Knyff's 80 HP Panhard—a new car with mechanically operated inlet valves—led, closely followed by Louis Renault with a new 30 HP 6.3-litre car. De Knyff's average was over 60 mph (96 km/h) and Renault was timed over a measured distance between Bonneval and Chartres at nearly 90 mph (144 km/h). There was furious overtaking amid the dust. Gabriel's Mors had passed 26 cars by the time he reached Chartres.

At Tours, Louis Renault led, but then Marcel Renault's 30 HP began to move into the reckoning. At Couhé-Verac he hit a drain while overtaking another competitor and the car overturned; Marcel died of his injuries. Reports began to come in of other accidents. Briton Claude Barrow and his mechanic were killed when their De Dietrich hit a tree at 80 mph (135 km/h) after colliding with a dog which jammed the steering. His team-mate Phil Stead was seriously injured in another crash. The Ulster driver Leslie Porter crashed his Wolseley and his mechanic Nixon

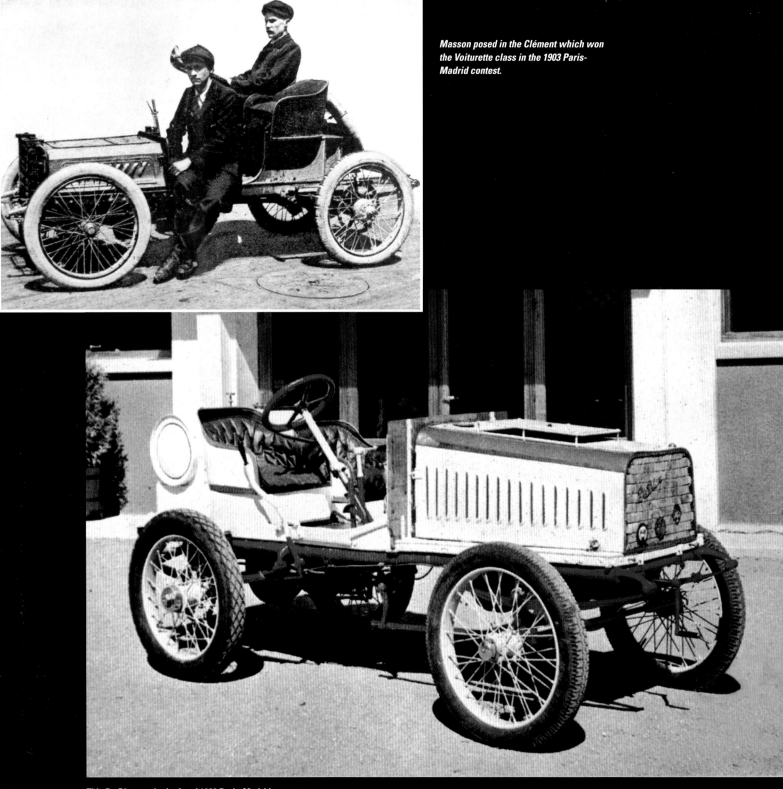

Masson posed in the Clément which won the Voiturette class in the 1903 Paris-Madrid contest.

This De Dion ran in the fated 1903 Paris-Madrid contest.

was killed. A woman crossing the road at Rambouillet was killed and Tourand, driving a Brouhout, crashed into spectators outside Angoulême trying to avoid a child on the road. The child, a soldier and his mechanic were killed.

Louis Renault was the first to arrive at Bordeaux, to be told of his brother's death. The third car home and the leader was Fernand Gabriel's 70 HP 11.6-litre Mors, averaging an astonishing 65.3 mph (105 km/h). The carnage of the day caused an immediate outcry. The French government dictated that the race should not go on to Madrid, an edict supported by the Spanish government. The cars' engines were not to be started again. The racers which arrived at Bordeaux were towed by horses to the railway station and returned to Paris on a freight train. An era had ended. The heroic days of racing from city to city over open roads were over. There had been 35 of these remarkable, brave and ultimately foolhardy races.

Arthur Duray, in a Gobron-Brillié, raised the Land Speed record to 84.73 mph (133.63 km/h), at Dourdan in 1903.

CHAPTER 3

The Gordon Bennett Flourishes and Fades: The Grand Prix Era begins

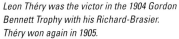

Leon Théry was the victor in the 1904 Gordon Bennett Trophy with his Richard-Brasier. Théry won again in 1905.

WITH Selwyn Edge's Napier win in the 1902 Gordon Bennett competition, the honour of organising the 1903 event fell to the Automobile Club of Great Britain & Ireland (ACGBI—soon to become the Royal Automobile Club). Racing on public roads was banned in England so a circuit in Ireland was chosen at Athy, County Kildare.

When this was announced, the ACF was scathing, regarding it as a poor substitute for the heroic open-road events. After the Paris-Madrid disaster, these comments were heard no more.

With the end of open-road racing the Gordon Bennett suddenly assumed new importance. In 1903 it became a proper international contest with three-car teams from Britain, France, Germany and the USA. When colours were allocated to the teams France again appeared in blue. There were loud voices calling for its cancellation after the Paris-Madrid, but the ACGBI persevered and the figure-of-eight circuit with one loop of 40 miles (64 km) and the other of 51 miles (82 km) was manned by 7,000 policemen to prevent any spectators straying on to the course. The total race distance was 327 miles (526 km).

The ACF selected de Knyff and Henri Farman with Panhards and Fournier with a Mors. All had competed in the Paris-Madrid. A week before the race Fournier was replaced by Gabriel, as Mors objected to his outside commercial activities. It seems that while the ACF nominated the cars, the choice of drivers was left to the manufacturers. The Mors had a distinctive body akin to an upturned boat and was known as 'Le Torpilleur'.

The opponents were a team of three 60 HP Mercedes, substituted at short notice after the team of 90 HP cars had

Leonce Giradot competed in the trials for the 1905 French Gordon Bennett team with his CGV.

been destroyed in a factory fire, three Napiers selected after competitive trials and two Wintons and a Peerless from the USA. At the technical inspection before the race de Knyff's car was found to be 31 lbs (14 kg) over the limit and some minor bits had to be removed. The French team was based aboard a ship, the 'Ferdinand de Lesseps', moored in Dublin harbour with all the equipment needed and with spare cars. Additional speed events in Ireland made up a week of sport.

The race on 2 July had an unexpected result. The 60 HP Mercedes led on all of the seven laps, despite being last-minute privately-owned substitutes. The winner was Jenatzy who was followed home by the Panhards of de Knyff and Farman while the Mors was fourth and the last finisher. De Knyff had lost time with an excursion off the road while the Mors had fuel starvation caused when the fuel filler loosened and the tank lost pressure. Two of the Mercedes dropped out, the Napiers crashed or were disqualified and the USA entries made no impression. The great days of Mors were ending with the pyrrhic Paris-Madrid the marque's last victory.

The failure to win the most important race now on the calendar smarted with the French. The ACF decided to hold trials to choose its entrants for the 1904 French Gordon Bennett team. The ban on racing was still in force, but after much negotiation it was lifted and a 58-mile (93-km) circuit in the Argonne hills, near the Belgian border, was chosen. The trials drew 29 entries from ten manufacturers.

The Panhards were the fastest cars, but when these suffered from overheating a new generation came to the fore. The trial was won by Léon Théry with a Richard-Brasier. His car had a 9.9-litre engine and chain drive and was built in a factory in Paris. It was notably lighter than some of its competitors. The second car was a Mors, a development of the 1903 cars, driven by Joseph Salleron. The third-placed car and thus the third string in the team was a Turcat-Méry in the hands of Henri Rougier. The Turcat-Méry came from Marseilles and was virtually identical to the De Dietrichs that also took part in the trial.

The Gordon Bennett, following the Mercedes win, had moved to Germany and was held on 17 June over an 87-mile (140-km) circuit outside the spa town of Homburg. With Kaiser Wilhelm II taking a special interest in the race, it was held under direct imperial patronage. The race attracted starters from six countries, including Italy which sent a team of Fiats.

Théry led from the start and gradually pulled away from Jenatzy's Mercedes. At the end of the race his lead was 11 minutes. To complete the French satisfaction and the spectating Kaiser's frustration, Rougier was third with the Turcat-Méry. Observers commented on the excellent roadholding and smoothness of the Richard-Brasier. Panhard's disappointment at its Gordon Bennett trials failure was somewhat assuaged a month later when Franco-American George Heath took his 90 HP 15.5-litre car to victory in the Circuit des Ardennes, leading home a similar Panhard driven by Teste.

The American millionaire William Vanderbilt Jr., who had driven in the Paris-Madrid, presented a cup to the American Automobile Association for a race to be held with similar rules to the Gordon Bennett but without limitation on the number of national entries. He stipulated that the race should be held in the United States. A course was chosen on Long Island on the outskirts of New York and the race held on 8 October. Despite Mercedes and Fiat entries, it was a French triumph. Only two of the 16 starters finished. The winner was the Panhard of George Heath with the Clément-Bayard of Albert Clément second. After the death of Marcel Renault, Louis Renault seemed to have lost interest in motor racing, but a single Renault ran at Long Island.

Jenatzy's electric-powered speed record was still standing. During the Nice Speed Week in April 1902 Léon Serpollet, in a steam car of his own construction, covered a flying kilometre in 75.06 mph (120.77 km/h). Later in the year in speed trials at Dourdan, south-west of Paris, Augieres in a 60 HP Mors pushed the record up to 77.13 mph (124.1 km/h).

The year 1903 saw two successful record runs, both by Arthur Duray in an unconventional Gobron-Brillié, which had two opposed pistons per cylinder. In his second run at Dourdan he raised the record to 84.73 mph (136.33 km/h). His team-mate Louis Rigolly brought the 13.5-litre Gobron out again for the Nice Week in March 1904, setting new figures of 94.78 mph (152.50 km/h). In July Rigolly took the Gobron to Ostend and there broke the record again with 103.5 mph (166.61 km/h).

Darracq, built at Suresnes in the northern suburbs of Paris, had been frustrated in the Gordon Bennett Trials, but Paul Baras took one of the Gordon Bennett rejects to the fast road outside Ostend and showed its performance, raising the record again to 104.52 mph (168.17 km/h). With its Gordon Bennett success and the fastest car in the world, the French motor industry could be satisfied at the end of 1904.

Théry's 1904 Gordon Bennett win placed the responsibility for the 1905 race on the ACF. A circuit was chosen at Clermont-Ferrand, the home of the Michelin tyre company which gave financial support. As in 1904, trials were held to choose the French team. There was loud grumbling from foreign competitors when the trials were held over the 85-mile (136-km) Clermont circuit on 16 June. Of the two dozen cars taking part the first three fastest over the course, the Richard-Brasiers of Théry and Callas and the De Dietrich of Duray, were selected.

The many rejects were unhappy. The ACF announced that a Grand Prix would be held on the circuit concurrently with the Gordon Bennett, allowing the first 18 cars in the trials to compete. Other nations would be restricted to six cars each. After much heated discussion this idea was shelved. The four-lap Gordon Bennett race was a triumph for Théry who led home two Fiats. His consistent times, perhaps with the help of his additional knowledge of the circuit, justified his nickname of 'The Chronometer'. A French team crossed the Atlantic for the Vanderbilt Cup in October and the journey was worthwhile as the Darracq of Hemery and the Panhard of Heath swept the board. Hemery had set a landmark for Darracq earlier in the year. He took a specially prepared 21.5-litre V-8 car to Arles and established a new record of 109.56 mph (176.43 km/h)

It was recognised that the Gordon Bennett had served its purpose as now there were too many manufacturers who

Victor Hémery set a Land Speed record of 109.65 mph (176.43 km/h) at Arles in 1905 in the 200 hp Darracq.

Francois Szisz, one-time chauffeur to Louis Renault and a factory test driver, won the 1906 French Grand Prix.

Left: The engine of the Renault which won the 1906 French Grand Prix was the first victorious Grand Prix power unit.

The Lorraine-Dietrich driven by Fernand Gabriel in the 1906 French Grand Prix broke down on its opening lap.

wanted to try their luck in international racing. The ACF announced that it would hold a Grand Prix in 1906 open to all manufacturers over a 64-mile (103-km) triangular circuit east of Le Mans. The race would be on two days with competitors doing six laps on each day, their times being aggregated.

Ten French manufacturers entered 25 cars. Mercedes sent a team of three and from Italy Fiat and Itala entered three cars each. The cars had to comply with the 1,000-kg weight limit. Circuit safety was paramount. Roads were lined with wooden palisades in the towns, pedestrian tunnels were built under the roads and to curb the dust some sections were tarred. Most teams raced in the now-recognised national colours though Renault, returning to racing again, appeared in red.

The 13-litre shaft-driven Type AK Renault dominated the race. Hungarian Ferenc (or Francois) Szisz—whose day job was foreman, doubling as test driver at the Renault factory—moved into the lead on the third lap and thereafter was never headed. Despite the tarring of the road, the field was plagued with tyre problems, probably exacerbated by the intense temperature of 35 degrees. Renault had the foresight to fit its three cars with detachable rims, a decision which probably decided the outcome as Szisz was able to change all four wheels in 3 minutes and 47 seconds. Speeds were rising. Over a measured distance Szisz was timed at 92 mph (148 km/h)

The start of the 1936 French Grand Prix at Montlhéry.

FRENCH GRAND PRIX

French manufacturers were frustrated by the rules of the Gordon Bennett Trophy which permitted only the limited entry of national teams of three cars. To give the nation's many manufacturers a chance of racing glory, the Automobile Club de France instituted the Grand Prix de l'ACF, better known as the French Grand Prix, in 1906.

The first such race, held over a long road circuit at Le Mans, was won by a Renault. Held again at Dieppe in 1907 and 1908, with Italian and German victories the G. P. was not the showcase the French manufacturers wanted and they lost interest. The race was not held again until 1912, when a Peugeot won at Dieppe, and again at Amiens in 1913. Held

under the threat of war, the legendary race at Lyon in 1914 saw a German Mercedes triumph over a strong Peugeot challenge.

The G. P. was revived in 1921. Until then it was 'the Grand Prix', a unique race, but others began to organise national events. Italian and Belgian races entered the calendar. Moving to various venues, the French G. P. was held for Grand Prix cars until 1928 but was then demoted to a humble sports-car handicap. Though it returned to its former glories in the early 1930s, the dominance of the German Mercedes-Benz and Auto Union teams caused a reappraisal and the G. P. became a sports-car race again in 1936 and 1937. It was a full Grand Prix again in 1938 and after World War 2 was revived in 1947.

In 1949 there were two races, a sports-car G. P. de l'ACF at Comminges and an F1 G. P. de France at Reims. In the 1950s and 1960s the races were held mostly at Reims, with occasional ventures at Rouen, both being traditional road circuits. Several races were held on the Charade circuit in the Auvergne, also a genuine road circuit akin to a mini-Nürburgring.

In 1968 the ACF gave up its organisation of the race, which then officially became the Grand Prix de France. It left the Charade in 1972, yielding to commercial pressure for shorter, more TV-compatible circuits. It moved to the Paul Ricard circuit in Provence, alternating with Dijon. Then in 1991 it was run on the short circuit at Magny-Cours, where it remained subsequently. Economic pressures caused a cancellation of the race in 2009 so the future of the first-ever Grand Prix was uncertain at this writing.

and his car was certainly capable of over 100 mph (160 km/h).

Murmurings that the Grand Prix was a pale imitation of the Gordon Bennett were forgotten. The ACF organised the race again in 1907, this time on a 47-mile (75-km) circuit outside Dieppe. The weight restriction was abandoned and replaced by a fuel-consumption limit of 9.4 mpg (30 litres/100 km). Unfortunately for French hopes it produced a foreign victory.

In the opening laps Duray in a Lorraine-Dietrich battled with Felice Nazarro's Fiat, but the Lorraine's gearbox broke so Szisz took up the battle. At the end the Fiat came home seven minutes ahead of the Type AK Renault, although there was some consolation as the next seven finishers were French.

The 1907 race had been a financial success and so it was repeated on the Dieppe circuit in 1908, but this time it was a disaster for the French. A Mercedes won and Benzes finished second and third. The fastest French car was the 14-litre Clement-Bayard with its overhead-camshaft engine.

The ACF and the French producers decided that there was no point in organising a race as a showcase for foreign manufacturers and so the Grand Prix was dropped in 1909. The decision affected many manufacturers. Clement-Bayard faded away as did Mors. Panhard never raced in top-flight events again and Renault disappeared from Grand Prix racing for 69 years.

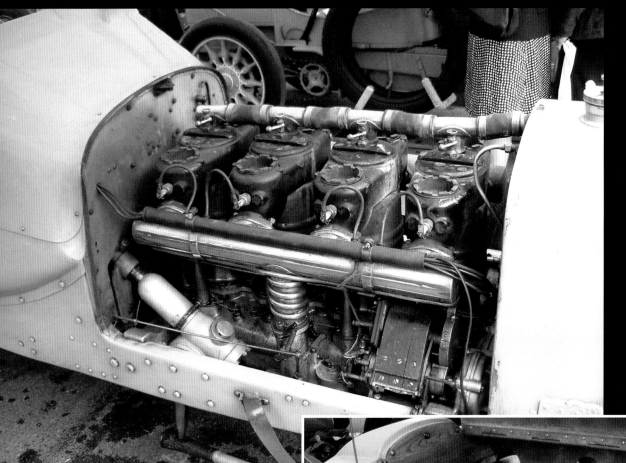

The engine of the 1906 French Grand Prix Panhard was a four-cylinder unit.

Copper water jackets are prominent in the engine of the 1906 French Grand Prix Mors.

CHAPTER 4

New Names, Smaller Cars:
Peugeot Triumphant

This Sizaire-Naudin competed at Brooklands in 1908.

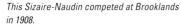

ALTHOUGH an era seemed to have ended, racing still flourished in France. The early distinctions between light cars and *Voiturettes* had become blurred. While the Grand Prix was a forum for the major machinery, the French magazine *L'Auto* saw the need for a class for smaller cars. It put up the Coupe de L'Auto in 1905. Virtually a reliability trial, it was limited to cars under 1,000 cc in 1905.

The first event was a flop, but when in 1906 larger engines were allowed the entry was better. The winner on a circuit at Rambouillet was a single-cylinder Sizaire-Naudin which had the innovation of independent front suspension. Another runner was a new marque, Delage. The Sizaire-Naudins, driven by M. Naudin and M. Sizaire, took first and second places in 1907 leading home an entry of 67 cars. *L'Auto* was fulfilling a need.

The racing of *Voiturettes* spread to Italy in 1907. Races at Turin and on the Madonie circuit, home of the Targa Florio in Sicily, saw victory for Lion-Peugeots. These were made at Beaulieu by nephews of Armand Peugeot who had broken away to form a separate company.

Realising the growing importance of the *Voiturette*, the ACF ran a race as a preliminary to the 1908 Grand Prix. Its regulations stipulated that engines should have bores not exceeding 65 mm for four-cylinder units while twins and singles had bores limited to 80 mm and 100 mm respectively. It was a win for a Delage with a two-cylinder De Dion engine; driver Albert Guyot having a non-stop run while his nearest rival, a Sizaire-Naudin, lost time refuelling.

The 1908 Coupe de L'Auto was run on a 31-mile (50-km) circuit at Compiegne. This time the Sizaire-Naudins had bigger tanks and ran non-stop. Naudin was first, Sizaire second while Jules Goux came third with a Lion-Peugeot. The flourishing class was encouraging both new marques and new drivers.

April 1909 saw the Lion-Peugeots in action again. Goux carried off a two-lap race on the 92-mile (148-km)

Madonie circuit. The limitations on bore size were producing bizarre engine designs, the winning twin-cylinder Lion-Peugeot having a capacity of 1,930 cc with a stroke of 192 mm (7.5 inches). Peugeot continued its success in the Coupe de L'Auto, running both singles and twins. Giosue Guippone won with a single which had six valves and an engine height of over 3 feet (1 metre).

These weird Lion-Peugeots continued to dominate the *Voiturette* class in 1910, but there was a sad set-back in the Coupe de L'Auto on the Boulogne circuit when Guippone was killed in practice, trying to avoid an errant cyclist, with a new VX5 sporting a stroke of 280 mm. A further disappointment for France followed when the race was won by a more conventional four-cylinder Spanish Hispano-Suiza.

In 1911 the AC de la Sarthe—which a decade later, as the AC de l'Ouest, was to institute perhaps the most famous motor race of all—organised a *formule libre* race on a circuit at Le Mans. Part of the 33-mile (54-km) circuit was later incorporated in the 24-hour-race course. Though still unwilling to relaunch the Grand Prix, the ACF encouraged this venture which was run as the G. P. de France.

A big entry faded away to a mere 14 starters on 14 July. Many were older Grand Prix cars, but amongst them was a tiny 1,327 cc T13 Bugatti, painted white as it came from Molsheim in German-controlled Alsace-Lorraine. Its constructor was expatriate Italian Ettore Bugatti, who moved from Italy to Germany as his career developed before establishing his own company in 1908.

The race began with a battle between a Fiat driven by Victor Hémery and a 1907 G. P. La Licorne in the hands of veteran Maurice Fournier. The front axle of the La Licorne broke and Fournier and his mechanic were killed when it went off the road. Hémery built up a commanding lead and went on to win, but the tiny Bugatti, driven by Ernest Friderich, Bugatti's right-hand man, scuttled round the course. In the intense heat it saw off the rest of the field to come second. A new name had appeared.

The 1911 Coupe de L'Auto, held again at Boulogne, drew 45 entries including a big British contingent. The regulations limited the engine capacity to 3.0 litres with restrictions on bores and strokes. Lion-Peugeot now had a V-4 engine while Delage opted for a more conventional 'four'. The two marques battled it out, the Delage of Paul Bablot winning from the Lion-Peugeot of Georges Boillot.

The manifest strength of the French industry made the ACF realise that it was time to promote the Grand Prix again in 1912. The Dieppe circuit was used and the regulations were simple, the only restriction being a maximum car width of 69 inches (1.75 m). There was a subsidiary class for 3.0-litre cars competing for *L'Auto* Cup, 42 of the 56 cars entered running in this lesser class.

Only three French manufacturers entered for the full Grand Prix: Lorraine-Dietrich, Rolland-Pilain and Peugeot. A Mercedes team was rejected by the ACF, perhaps still smarting from the 1908 defeat, on the pretext that the entrant was the Belgian agent and not the Stuttgart company.

After the Peugeot family made up their differences, Lion-Peugeot and the founding company had amalgamated. The company obtained the services of gifted Swiss engineer Ernest Henry who, guided by the experience of Boillot, Goux and Paul Zuccarelli—who had joined Peugeot from Hispano-Suiza—produced a revolutionary design which set the pattern for racing engines for the future. His 7.6-litre engine had two overhead camshafts and four inclined valves per cylinder.

The two-day race became a battle between the 15-litre Fiats and the L76 Peugeots, ending in a French triumph led by Boillot. The G. P. de France was held again in

Georges Boillot raced a Lion-Peugeot at Brooklands in 1909.

The first Bugatti in competition: Darritchon with a Type 13 at Gaillon in October 1910.

The engine of the Type 10 Bugatti marked the beginning of a legendary line.

GEORGES BOILLOT

Georges Boillot was born at Valentigney, Doubs in 1884. He worked for Lion-Peugeot as an engineer and raced its unorthodox tall single-cylinder cars, beginning with the 1908 Sicilian Cup. His first win was in the 1909 Normandie Cup at Caen, which he followed with victory in the 1910 Targa Florio. The Lion-Peugeot had become a V-4, one of which Boillot drove in the 1910 and 1911 Coupes de L'Auto taking second place in 1911.

When the Lion branch amalgamated with the main Peugeot company Boillot, with his fellow drivers Goux and Zuccarelli, began working with the designer Ernest Henry. The outcome was the superb 7.6-litre twin-cam G. P. Peugeot, a true landmark design. Boillot drove the car in the French G. P. at Dieppe and won. He pulled off a double in 1913. With a 3.0-litre Peugeot he won the Coupe de L'Auto on the Boulogne circuit, then went on to take a second Grand Prix win at Amiens. He took a 5.6-litre to the USA for the 1914 Indy 500 and led until a tyre burst and the chassis frame broke. He limped into 14th place.

The French ace's last race was the 1914 French G. P. at Lyon. The luxuriantly moustachioed Boillot duelled with the Mercedes team, holding the lead for much of the race until his Peugeot broke under him with a lap to go. In the early days of World War 1 Boillot was the personal driver of Marshal Joffre, the French commander-in-chief, but he transferred to the Armée de l'Air and became a fighter pilot. He was killed in a dogfight over Verdun in April 1916.

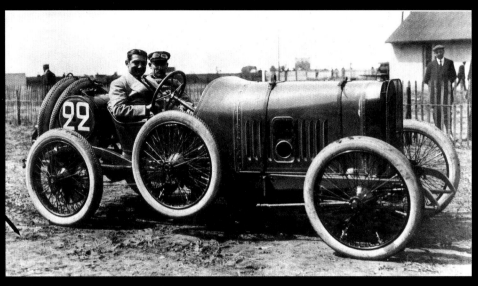
Georges Boillot in the 1912 Grand Prix Peugeot.

Georges's younger brother André was born in 1891. He too worked for Peugeot and drove exclusively for the marque. Doubtless inspired by his brother, André won the 1919 Targa Florio, the first major race to be run in Europe after World War 1. He went on to win the Coppa Florio in 1923 and 1925, also winning the Touring Car G. P., the curtain-raiser for the French G. P. in 1923 and 1925. His last major win was the Belgian 24 Hours at Spa, sharing the winning car with Louis Rigal. André was killed in a hill climb in 1931, driving an experimental 201X Peugeot which had an engine designed by Ettore Bugatti.

Georges Boillot drove the L76 Grand Prix Peugeot in the Mont Ventoux hill climb in 1912.

September and was another Peugeot win. Emboldened by these successes two L76 Peugeots crossed the Atlantic in the spring of 1913. Their destination was Indianapolis and the venture paid off, Goux winning the '500', refreshed by quaffing champagne at his pit stops, and gaining the first non-American victory.

Henri went back to his drawing board and produced two new designs for 1913. The Grand Prix regulations had changed, adopting a fuel consumption rule of 14.2 mpg (20 litres per 100 km). The result was a twin-cam 5.6-litre EX3, but for the Coupe de L'Auto there was a scaled down 3.0-litre version.

The designs did what was required. Boillot and Goux came first and second in the Grand Prix, held this time over a 19-mile (30-km) circuit at Amiens, though the win was marred as Paul Zuccarelli was killed when his EX3 hit a

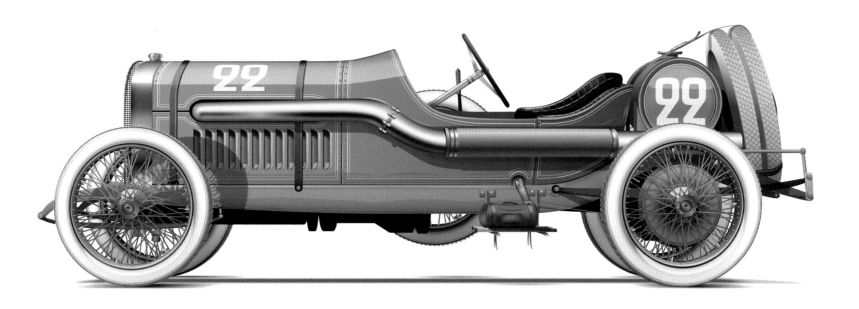

1912 L76 PEUGEOT

THE 1912 7.6-LITRE L76 PEUGEOT WHICH WON THE FRENCH GRAND PRIX DRIVEN BY GEORGES BOILLOT. ITS TWIN OVERHEAD CAMSHAFT
ENGINE ESTABLISHED RACING DESIGN PRACTICE FOR THE REST OF THE 20TH CENTURY.

farm cart while testing before the race. The 3.0-litre Peugeot carried the pair to another 1-2 in the Coupe de L'Auto at Boulogne in September 1913.

The Indy 500 venture must have been profitable as Peugeot returned there again in May 1914, sending two EX5s and a 3.0-litre. Delage, which had given a close race to the Peugeots in the 1913 Grand Prix, sent two of its Y-type 7.0-litre 1913 G. P. cars, developed by designer Arthur Michelat from his 3.0-litre Coupe racers. The race was a French battle. René Thomas took the flag in his Delage and collected $37,000 after Boillot, having shown that the EX5 was the faster car, retired with a broken chassis frame. Peugeot honour was upheld by the 3.0-litre which finished second.

A 23-mile (37-km) circuit at Lyon was chosen for the 1914 Grand Prix. The regulations were changed again with

engine size limited to 4.5 litres. It was a truly heroic race, held with the threat of impending war and with entries from all the major motor-racing manufacturers. From the 36 starters the race became a battle between Boillot's blue Peugeot EX5 and the white-painted Mercedes team. It had great national significance for the French with the deteriorating political situation and the memories of their 1870 defeat still fresh in many minds.

After five laps Sailer's Mercedes dropped out, leaving Boillot in front, where he stayed until lap 19 despite the harrying of the pursuing Mercedes. Both Peugeot and Delage had made a technical advance with front-wheel brakes which gave Boillot an advantage. The pressure was too much, though, and the Peugeot's engine broke leaving the Mercedes team to complete the 20th lap and take a 1-2-3 win, with Goux's Peugeot in fourth place. French

The 1913 Grand Prix Delage competed with Albert Guyot at the wheel.

A 'Brickyard' victory was the achievement of René Thomas, here in his Delage after winning the 1914 Indianapolis 500.

admissions afterwards were that the failure came through poor preparation and organisation. France had little time to dwell on her defeat as a month later Europe was at war.

There was a postscript. While Europe was locked in bitter conflict the USA was a non-belligerent observer, holding the 'Indy 500' in 1915. A few days before the war had begun a G. P. Mercedes of the Lyon team and one of the defeated Peugeots were shipped across the Atlantic. The pair did battle at the 'Brickyard' where the Mercedes, driven by Ralph DePalma, won again, leading the Peugeot of Dario Resta over the line by three and a half minutes. Resta returned to Indianapolis in 1916 and this time secured a Peugeot victory.

None of this concerned Georges Boillot, the defeated hero of Lyon, who, having become a fighter pilot, had been killed in action in April 1916. While Europe picked up the pieces after the war ended, the 'Indy 500' was revived in 1919, and the EX5 scored another victory in the hands of American Howdy Wilcox.

The 1914 Coupe de L'Auto was not held, but Peugeot had prepared a team of twin-cam four-cylinder 2,472 cc cars. Two of these went to Sicily in November 1919 for the Targa Florio, held on the notoriously testing Madonie circuit, made even worse by the autumn weather. Battling with the conditions and his rivals, André Boillot, the brother of Georges, came home the winner.

Exhausted at the end of the race, Boillot skidded and crashed into a grandstand within 30 yards (30 m) of the finish. He backed the car on to the road and reversed over the line. Told this was illegal, he drove back to the scene of the incident, turned the car round and crossed the line again to win. After that Peugeot virtually abandoned pure racing cars. Its competition forays of the 1920s were limited to sports versions of its production cars.

The Type 18 Bugatti was a hill-climb competitor before World War 1. This car, 'Black Bess', was owned by Roland Garros, the French World War 1 air ace.

André Boillot's 2.5-litre EX-6 Peugeot dropped out of the 1919 Indy 500 with 25 miles to go.

Jules Goux posed in the 1914 EX-5 Peugeot at Lyon before the French Grand Prix.

CHAPTER 5

The Twenties Begin to Roar:
The Rise of Delage

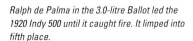

Ralph de Palma in the 3.0-litre Ballot led the 1920 Indy 500 until it caught fire. It limped into fifth place.

MOTOR racing in France was slow to start again after the war. The east of the country was in ruins, 1.7 million Frenchmen having died, and the nation was exhausted. It was over a year before the first race was organised. In 1914 the AC de la Sarthe had been about to promote the Coupe des Voiturettes for 1,400 cc cars when the war stopped everything. The club, now the AC de l'Ouest, organised the race again on 29 August 1920. It drew an entry of 26 cars, amongst which were three T13 Bugattis. The Bugattis were so dominant that Ernest Friderich won by a margin of 20 minutes.

Ernest Henri had left Peugeot in 1915. After working for other manufacturers on aero engines he joined Ballot at the end of 1918. Ballot had been founded in 1906 and was primarily an engineering company, but with the end of the war it moved into car manufacture.

Henri's first task was to design a car to race at Indianapolis in 1919. The handsome eight-cylinder 4.9-litre machine was designed and built in an amazing 120 days. The big Ballot was the fastest car at the 'Brickyard' but was unplaced after continuous tyre problems. It went to the 1919 Targa Florio where, in appalling conditions, it could not match the Peugeot.

The ACF announced that the Grand Prix would resume in 1921 and would be run to a 3.0-litre limit. Indianapolis jumped the gun, introducing this limit for the 1920 '500. Henri designed a straight-eight 3.0-litre Ballot, three of which ran at Indianapolis finishing second, fifth and seventh. Ralph de Palma had a two-lap lead with 13 laps to go when his engine caught fire.

The 1921 French Grand Prix was held at Le Mans on a circuit which would later be the course for the 24-hour sports-car race. French entries were Ballot, Mathis and Talbot-Darracq. The latter came from the French component of the Sunbeam-Talbot-Darracq Anglo-French combine and were virtually Sunbeams. The race had an unexpected outcome with an American victory, Jimmy Murphy's Duesenberg coming home 15 minutes in front of de Palma's Ballot after 321 miles (517 km) racing on a circuit which was rough, with broken stones in many places. Jean Chassagne's Ballot had led until its fuel tank split. A four-cylinder 2.0-litre Ballot was third, a prototype of a superb production sports car, the 2LS.

Italy decided that it could emulate the French. In September 1921 the first Italian G. P. was held over 20 laps of a 10.6-mile (17-km) circuit at Brescia. It was a Ballot triumph as Jules Goux led de Palma home. Two days earlier the 1,500 cc T22 Bugattis had taken the first three places in a *Voiturette* race on the same circuit. Bugatti had already scored in a *Voiturette* race at Garda in May 1921.

Meanwhile at Suresnes, the Paris works of the STD combine, a 1.5-litre *Voiturette* had been built with an engine which was virtually half of the eight-cylinder STD Grand Prix car. It was faster than the Bugatti so a showdown between the Talbot-Darracq and the Bugatti was expected in the Coupe des Voiturettes at Le Mans, ten days after the Brescia race. Ettore Bugatti, strongly suspecting what the outcome would be, scratched his cars, saying there was

insufficient time for preparation. The Talbot-Darracqs romped home in a 1-2-3 finish and repeated this a month later when the first 200-Mile Race was held at Brooklands.

Other developments in 1921 included a growing class for 1,100 cc cyclecars in parallel with the *Voiturette* class. The day before the *Voiturette* race at Le Mans, an 18-lap, 193-mile (310-km) cyclecar Grand Prix was held, which saw an easy win for a new name, Salmson. The first Salmson had been the spidery two-cylinder British GN, built under licence at Billancourt in the Paris suburbs, but it had grown into a miniature racing car with a twin-cam four-cylinder engine.

A race had been held in Corsica which was to be hugely significant. It was for four-seat touring cars with an engine capacity of 3.0 litres. Three French manufacturers entered teams: Chenard & Walcker, Bignan and Turcat-Méry. Victory went to a Bignan driven by Albert Guyot. This minor event in Corsica would lead to a huge and influential class of racing, growing to rival the Grand Prix world.

A similar car to this 1921 Grand Prix Ballot took second place in the French Grand Prix at Le Mans.

The Grand Prix formula was changed to 2.0 litres at the beginning of 1922. Three French manufacturers had cars at Strasbourg for the French G. P. in July 1922. Ballot produced a development of its 2LS sports car which had raced in the G. P. at Le Mans in 1921. Bugatti came up with a racing version of his eight-cylinder touring T30 and Rolland-Pilain had a relatively advanced left-hand-drive 'eight'. The Ballot and Bugatti had similar, cigar-shaped bodies, an early look at aerodynamics.

The 493-mile (793-km) race on an 8.3-mile (13.3-km) circuit, near Bugatti's factory, did not end in French celebrations as the race was dominated by a team of Fiats which were a great technical advance over the French products. Two Bugattis finished nearly an hour behind the winning Fiat. In September the Italian G. P., on a new track at Monza outside Milan, drew a huge entry of 39 cars. Fearing Fiat, only eight started, including the T30 Bugatti team. Once again the Fiats were unbeatable, but Vizcaya's Bugatti was third.

In the *Voiturette* class the Talbot-Darracqs were dominant, winning every race, but Fiat had produced a potent rival. Fear of defeat made the French team pick its races carefully to avoid a head-to-head contest. The 1.1-litre Salmson was developing rapidly and had no rivals amongst the cyclecars.

As a supporting race for its Grand Prix the ACF promoted an arduous touring car competition over 53 laps of the Strasbourg circuit. As well as having road equipment, the competitors had to comply with a fuel consumption rule of 15 litres per 100 km (11 mpg). Teams were entered by Voisin and Peugeot. Both were unusual as they had sleeve-valve engines. The race was a success for Voisin whose 4.0-litre cars took the first three places with Henri Rougier at the wheel of the winning car. André Boillot, who came fourth, finished with one and a half litres of fuel in his T174 Peugeot's tank.

Peugeot put its four-cylinder 3.8-litre T174 touring engine into a 1914 Coupe des Voiturettes chassis and took three of these cars to Sicily for the Coppa Florio, held on the Madonie circuit in November 1922. In the daunting Sicilian conditions, André Boillot gave Peugeot a win, finishing in front of a 4.9-litre Sunbeam driven by rising British ace Henry Segrave.

On 26 and 27 May 1923 a race was held that would have a profound effect on motor racing and its development. The AC de L'Ouest instituted the Le Mans 24-Hour race, using the same circuit as the 1921 French G. P., albeit with a slightly improved surface. The race drew 33 starters. Most of the French manufacturers with sporting aspirations were there, apart from Peugeot. The race, run in horrible weather conditions, was a battle between two Type U2 Chenard & Walckers and a British 3.0-litre Bentley.

The Bentley was quicker than the 3.0-litre overhead-camshaft Chenards, but was hampered by a lack of front brakes and in the later stages slowed by a leaking fuel tank. The Chenard driven by André Lagache and René Leonard came home in first place followed by the Chenard of Raoul Bachmann and Christian Dauvergne. A 2.0-litre Bignan was third ahead of the Bentley. Despite the conditions, a remarkable 30 cars finished the course. The race had been a success and would soon assume great significance.

The 1923 French Grand Prix was held in June on a 14-mile (23-km) circuit outside Tours. It drew entries from Bugatti, Delage, Rolland-Pilain and Voisin while foreign competition came from Fiat and Sunbeam. Bugatti and Voisin continued to explore the boundaries of aerodynamics. Bugatti used his T30 engine again, but it was covered by an all-enveloping body that was in some respects 30 years ahead of its time.

Gabriel Voisin was a visionary designer who came to motor racing from aviation. His G. P. car had a six-cylinder

These 1.5-litre Type 13 Bugattis dominated the Voiturette races at Le Mans and Brescia in 1920, becoming known as the 'Brescia' model.

version of his earlier sleeve-valve engine, set in a chassis and body that formed a semi-monocoque with an aerofoil shape. The rear track was narrow to enclose the wheels inside the bodywork.

Alongside these unorthodox machines the Rolland-Pilain was a development of the 1923 car, while Delage had returned to racing with a car designed by Charles Planchon, assisted by Albert Lory. It had a superb twin-cam V-12 engine in a conventional chassis.

The French contingent was outclassed by the Fiats and Sunbeams. The Fiats, aided by a new-fangled supercharger, were fast but fragile and the Sunbeams carried the day. A Bugatti was third and a Voisin was fifth. After the Delages fell out with broken connecting rods, a furious Louis Delage fired Planchon.

The French G. P. was supported by touring-car races which gave a clean sweep to Peugeot, who perhaps believed it was a better forum than an uncertain 24-hour race. The Type 174s took the first three places in the over-3.0-litre class and the 2.5-litre Type 176 did the same in the under-3.0-litre class. A month later the Rolland-Pilains went to a thinly-supported San Sebastian G. P. in Spain and took first and second places. Both Rolland-Pilain and Voisin crossed the Alps to Monza for the Italian G. P. in September, but the Fiats swept the board and after that both French marques faded from the racing scene.

In the history of motor racing there are seminal races which mark turning points in the sport. Amongst these were the 1914 French Grand Prix, the 1934 Eifelrennen and the 1965 Indianapolis 500. Another was the 1924 French Grand Prix. With symbolic significance, the race returned to Lyon. Bugatti produced an exquisite new car, the T35, which would become the backbone of racing for the next ten years.

Albert Lory, who had taken over the design office at Delage, had refined the V-12, while a new challenger, Alfa Romeo, came from Italy. Sunbeam came determined to repeat its previous year's success, also with a new car.

The aerodynamically advanced Type 32 Bugatti ran in the 1923 French Grand Prix at Tours. Although off the pace, one finished third.

The sleeve-valve-engined Voisin C3 Sport won the 1922 Touring Car Grand Prix at Strasbourg.

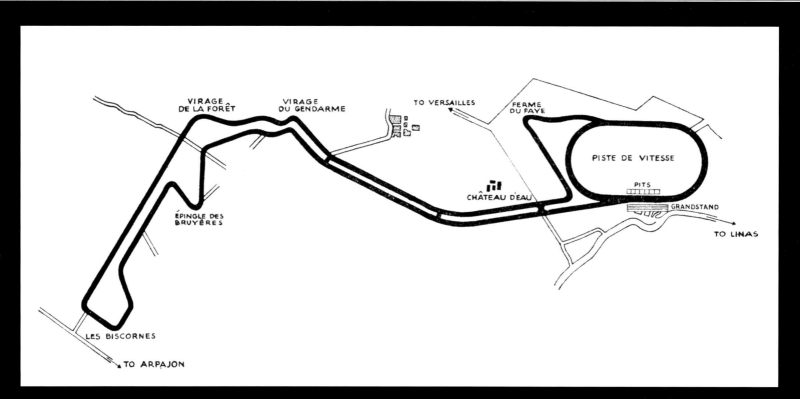

MONTLHÉRY

The Montlhéry track was the brainchild of Alexandre Lamblin, an industrialist who was also proprietor of the magazine *L'Aero Sports*. Lamblin had looked across the English Channel at Brooklands and, seeing its benefits, realised that France needed a test circuit. He instructed engineer Raymond Jamin to design an oval banked track for a site south-west of Paris. Jamin produced a 1.5-mile (2.5-km) track which was built and opened in 1924. During the following winter an artificial road circuit was added. This gave several variations of circuit with the longest, including half a lap of the track, measuring 7.8 miles (12.5 km).

The venue of the 1925 and 1927 French G. P.s, Montlhéry was also used for many other events in the 1920s. The banked track, designed for maximum speeds of 155 mph (250 km/h), became a magnet for record breakers. It saw successful attempts on the World Hour and 24-Hour records and countless assaults on other World and International class records. It was a huge asset for the French motor industry which used it for testing continuously. The French G. P. returned there in 1931 and every year from 1933 until 1937.

After World War 2 Montlhéry re-opened in 1948 but never quite rose to its former glories. For the faster cars the track had become unsuitable for record breaking, though many class records were set in the 1950s and 1960s until the banked concrete surface became too rough. The first major post-war race was a 12-hour sports-car event in 1948. In the following years there were minor races for Grand Prix cars, notably the G. P. du Salon and the Paris G. P. For French club and amateur drivers countless meetings were organised.

Montlhéry's principal race was the 1000 Kilometres for sports cars, held intermittently until 1994. To French delight there were wins for Matra in 1969 and 1970 and for Venturi in the last race in 1994. The surface continued to deteriorate to the degree that the course could only be used for historic events. At the end of 2005 it was closed and it seemed Montlhéry would be demolished, but at the end of 2008 plans were announced for its revival. Perhaps this most important site in French motor-racing history will have a new lease of life.

The supercharger was becoming a compulsory fitting, though eschewed by Bugatti and Delage.

In the race the pace was set by the supercharged Alfa Romeos, Fiats and Sunbeams. The Fiats dropped out with braking problems, the Sunbeams were delayed by faulty magnetos and a P2 Alfa Romeo won. The Delages of Albert Divo and Robert Benoist were second and third. The T35 Bugattis were plagued with tyre problems and failed to make an impression.

The defeat of French cars in the French G. P. came after another disappointment at Le Mans. A solitary Bentley wore down the teams from Chenard & Walcker and Lorraine-Dietrich to win. Three weeks after the Grand Prix, French prestige was somewhat restored when a 2.0-litre Bignan driven by Henri Springuel and Maurice Becquet won another newly-instituted 24-hour race, held in Belgium on a testing circuit at Spa-Francorchamps. A U2 Chenard & Walcker in the hands of Lagache and Leonard was second.

In September the Grand Prix circus moved on to the San Sebastian circuit in Spain. Alfa Romeo gave the race a miss but French hopes were dashed by Sunbeam, though

The 3.0-litre Chenard & Walckers dominated the first Le Mans 24-Hour race in 1923, coming 1st, 2nd and 7th. This is the 7th place car driven by Bachmann and Glazmann.

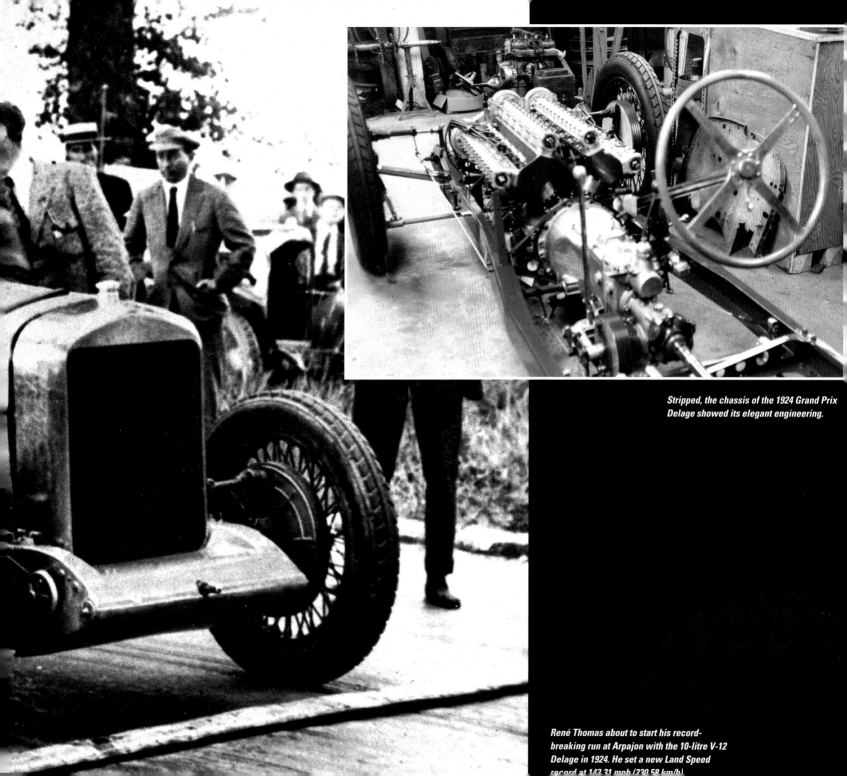

Stripped, the chassis of the 1924 Grand Prix Delage showed its elegant engineering.

René Thomas about to start his record-breaking run at Arpajon with the 10-litre V-12 Delage in 1924. He set a new Land Speed record at 143.31 mph (230.58 km/h).

Although it is the 'wrong' colour, the superb balanced lines of the Type 35 Bugatti are evident.

Right: Ernest Friderich passed the grandstands during the 1924 French Grand Prix at Lyon in his T35 Bugatti. He finished seventh in the debut of one of the greatest racing cars of all.

a T35 Bugatti driven by expatriate Italian Meo Costantini, the racing manager at Molsheim, now fitted with more enduring tyres, was second. The Delages of André Morel and Divo were the next finishers.

Cognisant that the Alfa Romeos were unbeatable, Bugatti and Delage stayed away from the Italian G. P. at Monza. The only French representatives were two Rolland-Pilains, now fitted with Schmid cuff-valve engines. They finished the race but at the tail of the field. In the *Voiturette* class Talbot-Darracq, spurred on by the fear of defeat by Fiat, had revamped their design so in 1924 the new car once again established dominance for the Suresnes factory.

There was similar 1.1-litre dominance for Salmson, whose car now had a much more mature chassis. A new French marque, Amilcar, had appeared but could not yet offer any challenge to the Salmsons.

Apart from its brilliantly designed—but as yet unsuccessful—V-12 G. P. cars, Delage had built a six-cylinder 5.1-litre car which appeared in hill climbs, setting records at Mount Ventoux and La Turbie in 1922, driven by René Thomas. In 1923 a 10.6-litre V-12 was built. Thomas took this to the speed trials on 6 July 1924 at Arpajon, on the N20, some 20 miles (30 km) south of Paris.

Thomas bravely took the big Delage along a narrow tree-lined road and through the flying kilometre at 143.31 mph (230.38 km/h), setting a new World Land Speed record. This was the last time the World record was held by a French car. It was broken a few minutes later by a 21.7-litre Fiat, which was seeking records at the same meeting.

The new Montlhéry banked track was used by Garfield and Plessier in May 1925 to take the World 24-Hour record in a 9.0-litre Type MC Renault.

CHAPTER 6

The First World Champions

The 1925 Grand Prix Delage was the winner of the French Grand Prix.

THE Targa Florio, the first major race of the 1925 season, was an all-French battle. Peugeot sent a team of Type 174s and Bugatti three of his new T35s. Peugeots led in the early stages but tyre failures impeded them and Costantini's Bugatti came through to win after five laps of the gruelling 67-mile (107-km) circuit. Wagner and Boillot followed in their Peugeots.

In May of 1925 Renault decided it was again time to garner some publicity with motor sports. A 9.0-litre Type MC driven by Repusseau won the Monte Carlo Rally. Next an MC was prepared with a four-seat touring body. This went to the purpose-built banked track at Montlhéry, a few miles from Arpajon, which had been opened the previous year. It took the World 24-Hour record, driven by American engineer Garfield and Robert Plessier at 87.58 mph (141.03 km/h).

Spurred by the success of their 24-hour race, the Belgians organised a full Grand Prix on the Spa circuit in June 1925. Alfa Romeo, Bugatti, Delage and Sunbeam entered. Sunbeam didn't appear, Bugatti said he could not afford to come, so three Alfas battled with four supercharged Delages. The latter all dropped out, leaving the Alfas victorious. They were so far in front that the drivers ate an impromptu meal from a table set in front of the pits.

The French G. P. a month later had a new venue, Montlhéry. This time all the teams were there, to race over 80 laps (621 miles/1,000 km) of the combined oval-track and road circuit. The Alfas were running away with the race when the leading car crashed, killing its driver Antonio Ascari. The Alfas were withdrawn from the race, which left the Delages battling with the Sunbeams. In drizzling rain, after eight hours of racing, the Sunbeams wilted and the Delages of Benoist and Wagner came first and second. The Bugattis, still disdaining superchargers, were not quick enough, but filled the next five places behind the surviving Sunbeam.

July was a good month for France. A 3.5-litre Lorraine-Dietrich saw off the Sunbeam and Bentley teams to win at Le Mans. The Delages didn't go to Monza for the Italian G. P. in September and so Alfas dominated the race. It had been announced that the Grand Prix formula for 1926 would be for 1,500 cc cars, so Bugatti used Monza as a try-out for its T39, a 1.5-litre version of the T35. It was successful and Costantini took third place.

The Alfas were not at San Sebastian for the Spanish Grand Prix, a fortnight after Monza, so Delage had a 1-2-3 success. It was marred as the fourth car of the team crashed and the driver, Paul Torchy, was killed. The rule that riding mechanics should be carried had been dropped at the beginning of the season, so—perhaps mercifully—Ascari and Torchy had raced alone.

The new 1,500 cc formula had little appeal for manufacturers. All withdrew from racing apart from Bugatti, Delage and Talbot-Darracq. Bugatti already had his T39 but Lory at Delage and the Italian Bertarione at Talbot were designing new cars. Both settled for supercharged straight-eight engines and low offset single-seater chassis.

Their designs taking longer than expected, only Bugatti was ready for the French G. P. at another new course, the oval, unbanked track at Miramas in the southern Camargue on 27 June. The race was a farce, the three Bugattis, now with superchargers, racing alone. Jules Goux was the winner, the other two cars being crippled by unsuitable fuel.

A cyclecar Grand Prix was held later on the same day. After the Grand Prix, Ettore Bugatti is said to have approached Emile Petit, the patron of Salmson, and suggested that it would be undesirable for the 1.1-litre Salmsons to put up a faster race average than the Bugatti. The Salmsons, supercharged for the first time, were up against a new Amilcar, the C6, a superb six-cylinder twin-cam design, but the C6s fell out and the Salmsons were able to ease off, saving Bugatti's face! Soon the C6 Amilcar would oust Salmson from its pre-eminent place amongst the cyclecars.

Bugatti still fought shy of the supercharger for his T35, but had enlarged the engine to 2.3 litres for non-formula races, making the T35T. These took a 1-2-3 in the Targa Florio, led by Costantini. The V-12 Delages were outpaced and insufficiently nimble on the tough circuit. The team was withdrawn from the race after Count Giulio Masetti crashed fatally.

Bugatti also produced the four-cylinder 1.5-litre T37, a small-engined version of the T35, intended mainly for the private owner. These were already appearing, especially in minor races. The T35 was in full production and 70 had found customers by the spring of 1926.

French blue was flying high in the summer of 1926. Lorraine-Dietrich took the first three places at Le Mans after the Bentley team retired in disarray. Renault returned to Montlhéry on 9 and 10 July with a special Type MC

fitted with a monoposto saloon body. Driven by Garfield, Plessier and Guillon, it recaptured the 24-Hour record which had been taken by Bentley. The new figure was 107.83 mph (173.64 km/h). Panhard, seeing Renault return to the fray, was not being left out of the chase for records. Shortly before the Renault success Ortmans took the World Hour record in a single-seat 6,355 cc sleeve-valve Type X-38 at 120.24 mph (193.46 km/h).

The Grand Prix at San Sebastian had been elevated with the title of European G. P. It saw the debut of the new Delages. They were faster than the T39A Bugattis, but the exhaust ran too close to the cockpit, burning the drivers. They made frequent stops to cool off, so Goux's Bugatti won, ahead of Morel's Delage and the Bugatti of Costantini.

The scene moved to England in August 1926 for the first British G. P. at Brooklands. There the Talbot 700 made its debut and showed it was a fast car, but there were teething troubles. All dropped out, one with a broken front axle. The Delage drivers endured by sharing cars and making frequent cooling stops. Senechal and Wagner came home first ahead of the privately entered T39A of Malcolm Campbell. The works T39As stayed at home.

Delage and Talbot abjured the Italian G. P. at Monza to develop cooler exhaust systems and stronger front axles. This left six starters and Bugatti ran away with the race, victory going to Jean Charaval who raced as 'Sabipa'. The result gave Bugatti the title of World Champion. A week later a *formule libre* race was held at Monza which drew an impressive entry. Two T35 Bugattis were entered, fitted with superchargers, thus becoming the T35C. These ran away with the race, Costantini leading Goux home.

In the autumn the 200-Mile Race was held at Brooklands. The Talbots, with strengthened axles, had a comfortable victory, coming first and second with Segrave at the wheel of the winning car. The C6 Amilcars outclassed the Salmsons in the 1,100 cc class and had done the same in other races in the latter half of the season.

There were no new entrants for the Grand Prix fields of 1927. It was evident that this branch of motor racing was fading away. Albert Lory reworked the Delage during the winter. He moved the supercharger, put the exhaust on the left side of the engine away from the driver's feet and fitted a sloping radiator cowl. From a mild ugly duckling he made

Lorraine-Dietrich publicised their win at Le Mans in 1925.

The 1.5-litre Type 37 Bugatti found a ready market among amateur racing drivers. This is the supercharged Type 37A version.

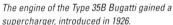

The engine of the Type 35B Bugatti gained a supercharger, introduced in 1926.

one of the most aesthetically satisfying Grand Prix cars of all time.

There were no significant changes to the Talbot 700 while Bugatti, knowing that the T39A had become a lost cause, did nothing. Interest was shifting to *formule libre* with a full calendar of races in France and Italy for which the popular and rapid-selling Bugatti T35B and T35C were ideal.

A new generation of drivers was emerging too, nearly all driving Bugattis. From Italy came the motorcycle aces Tazio Nuvolari and Achille Varzi. In France appeared Louis Chiron, who as a dance partner in the Hotel de Paris in Monte Carlo had persuaded one of his rich female customers to buy him a Bugatti and launch his career. 'Williams' concealed the identity of William Grover-Williams, a son of English parents, born in Paris. He had been chauffeur to Sir William Orpen, the famous artist, and had married Orpen's mistress. Orpen may have assisted his first racing ventures, but by 1927 'Williams' was in the Talbot team and also racing a T35 Bugatti.

The 1927 season began in March with a *formule libre* race at Montlhéry. Robert Benoist gave one of the G. P. Delages a preliminary canter and won by over three laps, a

foretaste of what was to come. Bugatti took three T35Cs to the Targa Florio and won yet again. Drivers were racing nearly every weekend. The Bugattis were the most frequent winners, partly by force of numbers, but there was opposition, especially in Italy from the P2 Alfa Romeos which had been unbeatable in 1924 and 1925.

A new Italian marque, Maserati, was beginning to be noticed in the 1,500 cc class. A name from the recent past appeared at Montlhéry in July in the Coupe de la Commision Sportive, a supporting race with a fuel-consumption regulation at the French G. P. meeting. André Boillot won the 248-mile (399-km) race in a Peugeot Type 176. He and Rigal had scored a win the previous year with a Type 174 in the Spa 24-Hour race.

The French Grand Prix, run at Montlhéry on the day after the supporting races, was a poor affair. The Bugattis were withdrawn so it was Delage vs. Talbot. Divo's Talbot led for a few laps, but the Talbots then fell out with mechanical bothers resulting in a Delage 1-2-3 led by Benoist. The sole surviving Talbot shared by 'Williams' and Jules Moriceau was fourth and last, nearly 40 minutes behind the winner. After their Montlhéry defeat the STD directors decided there was no point in spending money

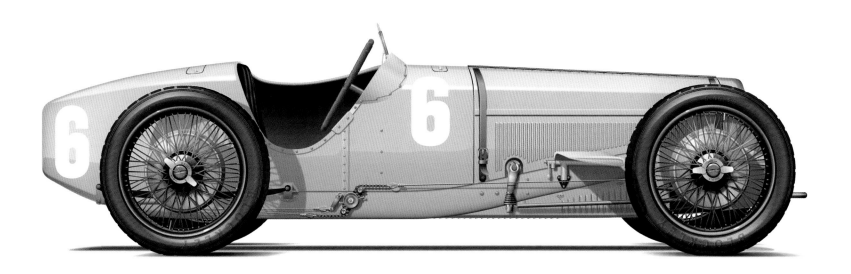

1927 GRAND PRIX DELAGE

IN 1927 THE 1,500 CC DELAGE WAS INVINCIBLE, WINNING THE WORLD CHAMPIONSHIP. THE DESIGN WAS SO ADVANCED THAT IT REMAINED
A RACING FRONT-RUNNER FOR TEN YEARS AND IT APPEARED IN FORMULA 1 RACES AS LATE AS 1950.

Robert Benoist competed in a 2.0-litre V-12 Delage at Gaillon in 1926.

ROBERT BENOIST

Robert Benoist has a place in motor-racing history as the first European Champion driver—the early equivalent of the World Championship. He was born in 1895, a son of the gamekeeper of the financier Baron de Rothschild. Benoist was a pilot in World War 1 and joined the Salmson racing team in 1921. After several successes in the cyclecar class he moved to the Delage Grand Prix team in 1924.

Benoist's first Grand Prix success was the 1925 French G. P. when he shared the winning car with Albert Divo. The 1926 season was difficult as the 1.5-litre Delage was hard to drive, overheating its drivers. It all came good in 1927 when Benoist and the Delage were an unbeatable combination. He won the French, Spanish, Italian and British G. P.s to become Champion and was appointed to the Legion d'Honneur.

Unlike the 21st Century, a European Champion received little financial reward in 1927. Benoist became manager of a Paris garage, had occasional drives for Bugatti and won the 1929 Spa 24 Hours in an Alfa Romeo. After that there was no racing until he joined the Bugatti team in 1934 and took over

management of the Bugatti showroom in Paris. His final success came in 1937 when he drove a T57G Bugatti to victory at Le Mans, sharing the car with Jean-Pierre Wimille.

Benoist was recalled to the French Army when World War 2 began. He was captured by the Germans in June 1940 while driving his T57 Bugatti road car. Ordered to join a German Army convoy, he accelerated up a side turning and escaped. He went to England where he joined the SOE. He returned to France as an agent in 1943.

With Wimille, Benoist joined a resistance cell led by former Bugatti driver 'Williams' and they carried out some successful sabotage operations. He took over command of the cell after 'Williams' was captured. Benoist himself was then captured but escaped, jumping out of a Citroën as he was being driven through Paris to the notorious Fresnes prison. Captured again after he was betrayed to the Gestapo, Benoist was executed in Buchenwald concentration camp in 1944. The first post-war motor race in 1945 was named the Coupe Robert Benoist in his honour.

Robert Benoist cornered his Delage at Miramas in 1927.

The 1.5-litre engine of the all-conquering 1927 Grand Prix Delage was justly considered a masterpiece.

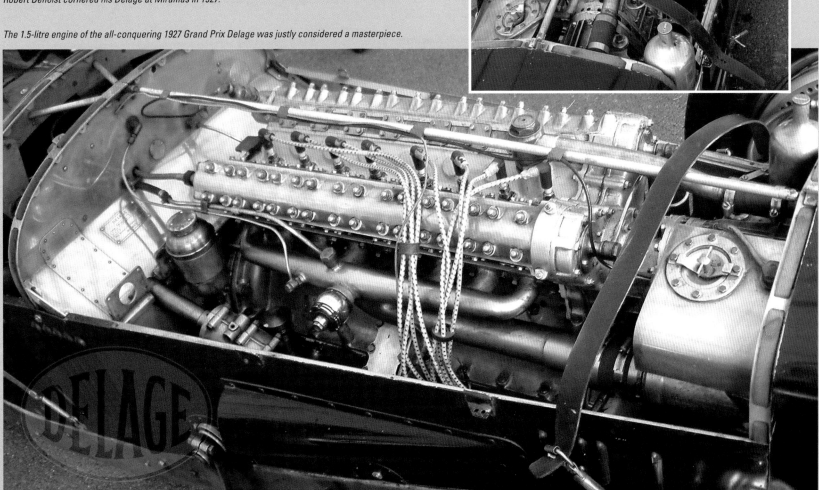

Salmsons of 1.1 litres nearly won the 1927 Le Mans 24-Hour race. This is the car of Casse and Rousseau which came third.

The 1927 Talbot 700s, never quick enough to challenge the Delages, later comprised the Scuderia Materassi in Italy.

on Grands Prix so withdrew the Talbot team from the sport.

A week after the French G. P., the G. P. de la Marne was held near Reims on the open plains of the Champagne district. The 4.8-mile (7.8-km) Reims circuit would become legendary. The winner was a newcomer in a T35B Bugatti, Philippe Etancelin, a Rouen wool merchant, who would himself become a legend with his turned-round cap and his wheel-sawing style.

Ettore Bugatti brought out his T39As for the Spanish G. P. at the end of July. The Bugattis went surprisingly quickly and Emilio Materassi's T39A even led Benoist's Delage for a few laps until he crashed. Benoist came home to win but Conelli on another Bugatti was second.

The Championship race at Monza in September drew a meagre field. Delage sent only one car for Benoist, who ran away with the race. The last round of the Championship was the British G. P. at Brooklands. There was a better field but inevitably the Delages were too fast for the rest. Benoist won, becoming European Champion with Delage. Bourlier and Divo took the places and Chiron in fourth was the best Bugatti. France honoured Benoist's feats when he was appointed a Companion of the Legion d'Honneur.

After the remarkable 1.5-litre Delages were sold to private owners at the end of 1927, three of the four cars came to England. The cars were in a different class from the other 1,500 cc machines and continued to gain successes in that class until the mid-1930s against the ERA and Maserati newcomers.

Richard Seaman, who had been the most successful *Voiturette* driver with an ERA in 1935, wanted a faster car for 1936. His mechanic Giulio Ramponi, who had worked for Alfa Romeo and Ferrari, suggested that Seaman should buy one of the Delages. Ramponi modified and updated it. Seaman dominated the 1,500 cc class in 1936, which led him to a seat with the Mercedes-Benz Grand Prix team.

Seaman sold the Delage to Prince Chula, the Siamese prince who was sponsoring and managing his cousin Prince Bira. Chula asked Albert Lory to update the chassis. A new frame was built with independent front suspension from a current road Delage. The venture was not successful, but the doughty Delage was raced by other drivers after World War 2 and last appeared in a Formula 1 race in 1950, 24 years after its debut.

French efforts in sports- and touring-car races disappointed in 1927, though it was a close thing at Le Mans. The larger cars were absent, but the three cars of the Bentley team were involved in a crash at dusk. Two were eliminated but the third car, badly damaged, limped on to the finish to win after a 3.0-litre Aries had fallen out. Finishing behind the Bentley—and waiting for it to fail—were two 1.1-litre Salmsons.

Voisin went after records at Montlhéry in the summer of 1927 with an eight-cylinder 7.9-litre sleeve-valve car with a racing two-seat body. Driven by César Marchand, Yves Morel and Kiriloff, it took a clutch of World and class records, finishing triumphantly with the 24-Hour record at 113.4 mph (182.46 km/h).

In 1936 the 1.5-litre Delage was driven by Dick Seaman, still fast enough to dominate the Voiturette class.

Independent front suspension was fitted to the 1.5-litre Delage in 1937 in a vain attempt to keep it competitive.

CHAPTER 7

Bugatti Triumphant

The 1.5-litre engine of the unsupercharged Bugatti Type 37.

THE 1,500 cc Grand Prix formula was abandoned at the end of 1927. It had become virtually moribund when Louis Delage followed Talbot in announcing he was withdrawing from racing, as the cost had brought his company close to bankruptcy. The formula was replaced by a weight limit, but this was almost universally ignored in 1928 and used only in the Italian Grand Prix.

Single-seater racing became largely a *formule libre* free-for-all in which Bugatti was ideally placed. The T35B and C offered a competitive racing car for customers who could race it anywhere and at the highest level. For the less ambitious there was the 1.5-litre T37 and its supercharged variant, the T37A. By the time production finished in 1931 some 215 racing versions of the T35 series had been built and some 290 T37s and T37As had found customers.

On the tracks they faced little opposition. England was only making sports cars. In Italy there were only two or three examples of the P2 Alfa Romeo, which was possibly quicker than the Bugatti. The sports 6C 1750 Alfa Romeo offered little opposition and Maserati was only making 1.5-litre cars in minuscule numbers.

The 1928 season opened with a clutch of Italian races of which Tazio Nuvolari won three with a T35C Bugatti. At the beginning of May the Bugatti works team went to its fiefdom of the Targa Florio, but were amazed when the first three laps of the five-lap race were led by a woman driver from Czechoslovakia, Elisabeth Junek, inevitably driving a T35B Bugatti painted yellow and black. She was denied a remarkable victory by a leaking water pump. Albert Divo, now driving for the Molsheim factory, was the winner.

The availability of a front-line racing car was bringing more women into the sport. Two weeks after the Targa Florio the French driver Janine Jennky, who was the mistress of Albert Divo, scored a notable win with a T35C in the four-hour Coupe de Bourgogne at Dijon. Remarkably the 1,500 cc class was won by another woman, Lucy Schell, with a T37A Bugatti. A decade later

Mme. Schell would have an influential place in French racing.

Louis Chiron was rapidly emerging as the top French driver. He was the number one of the Bugatti team and also drove a T35B owned by Alfred Hoffmann, the heir to the Hoffmann-La Roche pharmaceutical empire. As a bonus Hoffmann's wife Alice became Chiron's mistress. Showing his skill and the dominance of Bugatti, Chiron went to Rome in June for the Premio Reale di Roma, run on an 8-mile (13-km) circuit outside the city. All the leading Italian drivers were there but the works T35C Bugattis of Chiron and Gaston Brilli-Perri came first and second.

STD sold its Talbot 700 team to the Italian Emilio Materassi as a package. Materassi had a full season with the cars. He won the 1,500 cc class at Alessandria, then scored an outright win early in May, beating the Bugattis and sundry Alfas and Maseratis in the Circuit of Mugello, run over six laps of a tough and demanding Madonie-like 38-mile (61-km) course in the mountains north of Florence. Luigi Arcangeli used one of the Talbots in the Circuit of Cremona, five laps of a massive 40 mile course,

and won again, finishing in front of Nuvolari's T35C Bugatti. Returning from Rome, Chiron dominated the Marne G. P. at Reims then went to San Sebastian and repeated the performance in an all-Bugatti field.

The Talbots were still going well. In mid-August it was Materassi's turn to beat Nuvolari into second place in the Circuit of Montenero, near the seaport of La Spezia. The only race run to the Grand Prix formula was the European G. P. at Monza, early in September. This drew a big field from which 21 cars started.

Immediately it became a wheel-to-wheel battle between the Bugattis and the Talbots, with Varzi intervening in a P2 Alfa. Materassi was running fifth amongst the leading group when he came up to lap two slower cars. It seemed they touched and the Talbot somersaulted into the crowd, killing Materassi and 22 spectators. The race continued, only Chiron and Varzi continuing to battle for the lead. When the chastened drivers finished the 60 laps, Chiron was the winner followed by the P2 Alfa and Nuvolari's Bugatti.

Czech driver Elisabeth Junek was perhaps the greatest woman racer of all. She is with her Type 35B Bugatti after winning at Montlhéry in 1927.

From the starting grid of the 1928 Boulogne Grand Prix, a typical provincial race, the winner was Delage number 19 of Malcolm Campbell. Number 26 was a Corre-la-Licorne and number 27 a TAM.

Apart from the successes of the ill-fated Talbots in Italy, the 1,500 cc class had seen almost continuous Bugatti wins. In England Malcolm Campbell won the 200-Mile Race at Brooklands with a T39A, then bought one of the all-conquering Delages. Taking this to the Boulogne G. P., Campbell won the 278-mile (447-km) race by a margin of more than an hour.

There were fewer races for the 1,100 cc cars which had grown up and now scarcely deserved to be called cyclecars. It was still an all-French contest between Salmson and Amilcar, but the more advanced C6 Amilcars were getting the upper hand. At the Boulogne meeting the 1,100 cc race was won by new Amilcar driver José Scaron, who would soon dominate the class.

Apart from Bugatti the French manufacturers seemed to have lost interest in sports-car racing, although this branch of the sport was flourishing. At Le Mans no challenge was offered to the Bentleys and it was the same in the Spa 24 Hours where an Alfa Romeo won. At the beginning of the 1928 season Ettore Bugatti signed Tazio Nuvolari as a works driver. His first drive was in the Mille Miglia, the 1,000-mile race around Italy from Brescia to Rome and back again. Nuvolari led a team of three sports T43 Bugattis, which had the T35B engine in a longer chassis. The trio battled with the Alfa Romeos for the lead, but fell back after Rome.

Soon afterward Nuvolari had a fierce row with Meo Costantini, the Bugatti manager, about race entries and the deal ended abruptly. Nuvolari took the path to Enzo Ferrari's Alfa-racing Scuderia. The French G. P. had reached a nadir, run as a sports-car handicap at Comminges in south-west France. If the intention was to encourage manufacturers, it failed. 'Williams', now a member of the Bugatti team, beat a field of 1,100 cc sports cars with a road-equipped T35C.

Germany, emerging from the financial cataclysm which followed the war, in 1928 held its G. P. at the newly built Nürburgring. It was a sports-car race using the whole 17-mile (27-km) circuit with the major performers the works-entered 7.1-litre Mercedes-Benz SS models. Bugatti sent two T35Bs and two T35Cs, fitted with wings and lamps. These were supported by private entrants including Mme. Junek, sharing driving with her husband. The Mercedes were too fast for the Bugattis and won the race. The best Bugatti was Brilli-Perri in fourth place while Chiron was sixth. Sadly Mme. Junek's husband overturned their T35B and was killed, bringing her immediate retirement from racing.

Ignoring the success of those races which refused any rules, for 1929 the AIACR introduced a new Grand Prix formula. It relied on a fuel-consumption limit, 14 kg per 100 km (c 14.5 mpg). In a bizarre quirk the fuel had to be carried in an exposed cylindrical tank sporting a large fuel gauge. Apart from two races, this requirement was ignored.

Despite the tragic death of Materassi at Monza, the Talbot 700s continued to race as the Scuderia Materassi. With a 700 Gaston Brilli-Perri took the first important race of the season at Tripoli. In April another legendary race, the Monaco Grand Prix, was inaugurated, racing through the narrow streets of Monte Carlo. This saw a victory for 'Williams' in his green-painted T35B Bugatti, after a long battle with Rudi Caracciola's SSK Mercedes.

A pattern was becoming established, with races almost every weekend in France or Italy. Bugattis dominated the French races while the P2 Alfas and the rising Maseratis were hard to beat on their home ground. The Bugatti hold on the Targa Florio continued with victory going to Albert Divo. In June Brilli-Perri took another win for the Talbot 700, now painted red, in the Circuit of Mugello.

The French G. P., run to the fuel-limit formula over 37 laps of the 24-hour circuit, produced a surprising entry of two Type 174S Peugeots. With one of these Andre Boillot almost upset the Bugatti applecart. He battled all the way with 'Williams' and held the lead for several laps. 'Williams' won but Boillot took an impressive second place in front of the works Bugattis of Conelli and Divo.

It was an indication of the strength of racing that a week later Grands Prix were held both at Reims and Dieppe and both drew big fields, mainly Bugatti, with 12 at Reims and 17 at Dieppe. Each saw Bugatti successes as Etancelin won at Reims and a rising driver, René Dreyfus, took the flag at Dieppe.

The German G. P. was again run as a sports-car race on the Nürburgring. Bugatti wanted to avenge the defeat of the previous year, especially as the race was run on Bastille Day. Chiron did what was required. He chased Caracciola's Mercedes until that expired and went on to victory in his T35B, quaffing champagne at his pit stop en route. 'Phillipe', otherwise the banking heir Phillipe de Rothschild, was second in another T35B. The second race run to the fuel consumption formula was at San Sebastian in Spain. Chiron and 'Phillipe' repeated their German success by taking first and second places.

While Bugatti was blazing the glory of French Blue around the circuits, Le Mans had been, once again, a Bentley benefit, and 6C 1750 Alfa Romeos had dominated the Spa 24-Hour race. The Italians didn't like the consumption formula so abandoned the usual Grand Prix at Monza and ran a three-heat and final *formule libre* race at the track instead. In the final the lead changed constantly, in a manner which was to become the norm at Monza over the years. The Talbot 700s of Arcangeli and Nuvolari battled for the lead. Finally Varzi took the race in a P2 Alfa, setting an impressive average speed of 116.68 mph

(187.73 km/h). Not far behind, the Nuvolari Talbot was second.

In October of 1929 the Wall Street crash was the most dramatic sign of an economic crisis that had been looming during the year. It has been suggested, cynically, that the rich are never richer than when the poor are poor, the slump hitting hardest for those at the bottom of the ladder. The motor-racing world, though affected, still carried on much as before. France, although seeing a decline in industrial production and a rise in unemployment, suffered less than the United States, Britain and Germany.

By 1930 the T35 Bugatti had been raced for seven seasons while the T35B and C versions were starting on their fifth season. With little opposition and continuing success there had been no need for major developments and improvements. By the beginning of 1930, 191 racing T35s had been built and sold. It all changed in 1930 when Alfa Romeo put the splendid P2 engine into a new chassis and Maserati, maturing all the time, developed its Type 26 into a very quick and competitive 2.5-litre machine.

At Monaco Dreyfus won after Chiron was slowed by a problem with his throttle linkage and all the finishers were Bugattis, but in the Targa Florio Varzi's P2 Alfa beat Chiron and Divo, despite his riding mechanic having to beat out the flames when their car caught fire on the last lap. In Rome Arcangeli, with a new Maserati, beat Chiron by a length after 160 miles (257 km).

Anglo-French driver William Grover-Williams, alias 'Williams', won the first Monaco Grand Prix in 1929. An SOE agent in World War 2, he was executed by the Nazis.

André Boillot in a Type 174S Peugeot—fitted with the tank and fuel gauge required by the rules—gave the Bugattis some opposition in the Grands Prix of 1928-1930.

ETTORE BUGATTI

Bringing unique artistry to car design, Ettore Bugatti became a world-famous legend in his lifetime. An Italian by birth in 1881, he was the son and brother of highly acclaimed artists. After an apprenticeship in Milan, Bugatti moved to German-held Alsace where he worked for De Dietrich, producing the De Dietrich-Bugatti. His entry for the 1903 Paris-Madrid race was rejected, ironically on safety grounds owing to a peculiar driving position.

Bugatti went on to design cars for Mathis and Deutz before establishing his own company at Molsheim in 1909. The Bugatti quickly gained a reputation as a sports and competition car. World War 1 forced Bugatti to flee Molsheim, but he designed and built aero engines in Paris that were destined to influence the Duesenberg brothers in America.

Returning to Molsheim after the war, Bugatti found Alsace now a French department. He began producing touring cars with a sporting element and entered the Grand Prix field. The first G. P. Bugattis in 1922 and 1923 were more bizarre than successful but his T35, which appeared in 1924, was one of the all-time great racing designs. The T35 and its developments dominated racing in the late 1920s and became the first production racing cars for sale to customers.

In the early 1930s Bugatti gradually handed over car design to his son Jean. There was some conflict when Jean's ideas embraced design developments which went against the grain

Ettore Bugatti pictured in 1908.

of the conservative Ettore. He became involved in other projects including high-speed railcars, the production of which helped to keep the company afloat.

Bugatti was now recognised as a major manufacturer of luxury cars, among which the T57 was considered one of the most desirable cars in the 1930s. Although Bugatti was no longer a power in the Grand Prix world, racing versions of the T57 won the Le Mans 24 Hours in 1937 and 1939.

Bugatti ran his company as a paternal autocracy, riding around the Molsheim estate on his horse, wearing his customary bowler hat. Disillusioned and deeply hurt by a workers' strike in 1936, he moved from Molsheim to Paris, where he produced a stream of designs for boats, aircraft and other devices. The death of Jean in a road accident in 1939 was a huge blow, but the company was saved from impending financial disaster and perhaps closure by the outbreak of World War 2. Bugatti was forced to turn the Molsheim factory over to the occupying Germans.

After the war the factory was requisitioned by the French government following suggestions that Bugatti had collaborated with the enemy. Ettore was striving to regain possession of his factory when he died after a stroke in 1947. The cars he designed and produced became recognised world-wide as motoring icons, highly prized by collectors.

The European G. P. at Spa was the only race run to the consumption formula in 1930. The works Bugattis, again with the ugly outside tanks, faced a thin, motley field apart from a Type 174S Peugeot driven by Henri Stoffel. The Bugattis had various problems while Stoffel kept going. In second place at the start of the last lap, sadly Stoffel ran out of fuel halfway round which let the Bugattis take a 1-2-3. The finish was not popular with the crowd as Guy Bouriat, who had been leading, stopped before the line to let the team's lead driver, Chiron, take the flag, accompanied by booing and catcalls.

The Monza G. P. stood in for the Italian G. P. and was run in heats and a final. It was a sign of the times that it was a Maserati 1-2-3 with the best Bugatti driven into fourth place by Giovanni Minozzi.

The French G. P. came at the end of 1930 as a *formule libre* race. It must have been a relief to the French drivers and entrants that the Italians stayed away. Run at Pau, near the Spanish frontier, it narrowly avoided another blow to French pride. On the last lap of the 25-lap race over a

9.8-mile (15.7-km) circuit, the works Bugattis had dropped out and 'Phi-Phi' Etancelin led from the sports 'blower' Bentley of the English driver Tim Birkin. Etancelin needed a fuel stop that would have let Birkin through, so he kept going. His T35C just reached the flag before his fuel ran out. Already at Le Mans, there had been no French opposition to the Bentleys.

There had been huge operatic-style dramas in Italy. Varzi, who loathed Nuvolari, had been unwilling to stay with him in the Alfa team, so had gone to Maserati in mid-season. In the last major race of 1930, the Spanish G. P. at San Sebastian, the Maseratis of Varzi and Aymo Maggi were first and second. The Bugatti team was in disarray, so the Peugeots of Stoffel and René Ferrand took most creditable third and fourth places.

Ettore Bugatti knew he had work to do. If Peugeot had taken Grand Prix racing seriously instead of competing with tuned sleeve-valve touring cars, the French Racing Blue story could have been different.

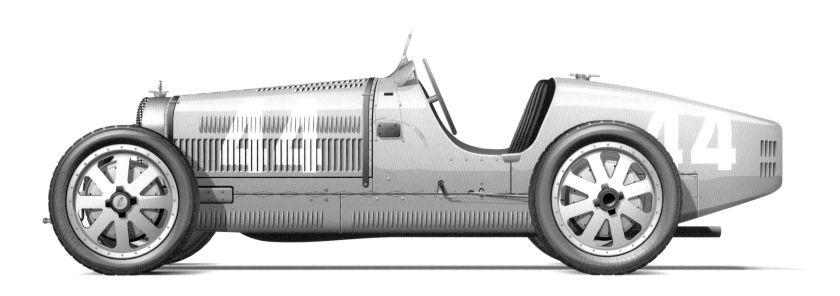

1930 TYPE 35B BUGATTI

THE FIRST GRAND PRIX CAR SOLD TO CUSTOMERS, THE 2.3-LITRE TYPE 35B BUGATTI WAS THE BACKBONE OF GRAND PRIX RACING IN THE
LATE 1920S AND EARLY 1930S, SCORING INNUMERABLE WINS FOR THE WORKS TEAM AND FOR PRIVATE ENTRANTS.

AMILCAR
PARIS

Seen at Brooklands, the very rapid 1.1-litre Amilcar C6 was popular with British drivers. Goldie Gardner, who later achieved fame as a record breaker, was at its wheel.

Though fast, the Type 43 Bugatti achieved no major success in sports-car races.

By the late 1920s French hopes of a Le Mans win had dimmed. This 1.1-litre Tracta, unusual with front-wheel drive, was among the runners in 1929. It finished in 10th place.

CHAPTER 8

A Fading Blue

IN 1929 American racer Leon Duray—whose real name was George Stewart—brought two front-drive Miller 91s to Europe. Designed for US track racing with advanced centrifugally supercharged twin-overhead-camshaft engines, the Millers were much faster than any European 1.5-litre car. Duray had a mixed season at the end of which, knowing the Millers would be obsolete in the US after a rule change, he did a deal with Ettore Bugatti who took the Millers in exchange for three sports T43 Bugattis.

The Miller engines and their front-wheel drive fascinated Bugatti. He and his son Jean studied the straight eights and designed a twin-camshaft development of the T35 engine which appeared early in 1931 as the T51. Apart from the engine the rest of the ex-T35 was unchanged, showing how advanced the design had been in 1924. To drive the T51, Chiron was retained and Varzi was tempted away from Maserati, perhaps with the offer of a red-painted T51 to drive in the races where the works cars were not competing.

Maserati had made further development of its 2.5-litre Type 26 while Alfa Romeo had produced a new 2.3-litre eight-cylinder model which could be either a sports car or a pure racing car—so the T51 faced strong rivals. These all raced under a new Grand Prix formula which was simple:

the cars had to have two seats and the races had to be of 10 hours duration.

The season began well for France. Varzi won with the red T51 at Tunis and at Alessandria in Northern Italy while Chiron was the winner at Monaco. The Targa Florio was run in heavy rain which turned the roads into quagmires. Varzi was beaten by his hated rival Nuvolari whose new Alfa had front mudguards which protected the driver.

The first race run to the formula was the Italian Grand Prix at Monza in May. It was a bad Bugatti day. The new Alfas were uncatchable and finished first and second. The best T51 was third, driven by Divo and Bouriat. The 8C Alfa Romeo thereafter became known as the 'Monza' model.

For Bugatti there was another setback. The string of Bentley wins at Le Mans had rankled. Bugatti persuaded Michelin to sponsor a team of three sports-racing 4.9-litre T50s. One, entered for the Mille Miglia in April driven by Varzi, retired soon after the start. The team of three, surprisingly painted black, arrived at Le Mans with high hopes. The race was a disaster. The Michelin tyres were not up to the task and in the early laps all the T50s threw tyre treads. Worse still, when a tyre burst Rost's car ran off the road hitting some spectators and killing one. The team was

Achille Varzi took his Type 51 Bugatti round the station hairpin at Monaco in 1931, finishing third. This section of the circuit has changed little in 80 years.

withdrawn from the race and an Alfa Romeo swept on to victory.

A week later at Montlhéry, in the 10-hour French Grand Prix, Bugatti turned the tables on Alfa Romeo after Michelin tyres had been discarded in favour of Dunlops, rushed from England. The Alfas had persistent brake problems and the T51 shared by Chiron and Varzi carried the day.

In the middle of July the Grand Prix circus moved to Spa for the Belgian Grand Prix, another 10 hour marathon. This time it was the turn of 'Williams' and Caberto Conelli to score a T51 victory, gained in part by quicker pit work and fewer stops, beating the best Monza Alfa by nearly a lap.

The German economy was improving. Having missed 1930, the German G. P. was staged again in 1931 at the Nürburgring. The race was run in heavy rain. To German delight Caracciola coped better with the conditions in his SSK Mercedes and could not be caught by Chiron and Varzi. It was a sign of the times that Etancelin, previously a loyal Bugatti customer, had bought a Monza Alfa in mid-season.

Bugatti realised that he needed a more powerful car. The result was the T54, produced allegedly in 13 days. A 4.9-litre T50 engine was fitted to the chassis of a T47, an abandoned sports-car project. With a body similar to the T51 this was a powerful but nose-heavy ill-handling car.

Two were taken to the Monza G. P. to be driven by Varzi and Chiron. The race was run in heats and a final with the major opposition a 12-cylinder Alfa Romeo and a 16-cylinder Maserati. The T54s came first and second in their heat but were slowed in the final by thrown tyre treads.

There was consolation at Brno, in Czechoslovakia, the last big race of the 1931 season. On the opening lap Fagioli in a Maserati knocked down a footbridge crossing the track. Several cars were eliminated in the resulting chaos but

The engine of the Type 47 Bugatti.

The engine of the Type 51 Bugatti was introduced in 1931 as a twin-cam development of the Type 35, strongly influenced by the American Miller.

Chiron avoided the wreckage in his T51 and went on to win.

At the beginning of 1932 it seemed that Bugatti would still be competitive with his T51. Varzi won in Tunis but the Monza Alfas were the victors at Monaco and in the Targa Florio. Then, at the beginning of June, a bombshell burst on the Grand Prix world. For the Italian G. P. Alfa Romeo produced a new racing concept, the monoposto Type B. This made all existing Grand Prix cars obsolete. For the rest of the season the Bugattis now could only be a supporting cast.

It was the same in sports-car racing, with the 2.3-litre 8C Alfas winning everywhere. A new sports Bugatti, the T55 with a T51 engine in a long chassis, had failed at Le Mans while a revolutionary machine, a four-wheel-drive T53 Bugatti with the 4.9-litre engine—perhaps derived from study of the Miller 91s—had been withdrawn at Monaco, though this was gaining successes in hill climbs.

Away from the circuits a modest restoration of French pride was manifest. The British driver George Eyston, who had gained a big reputation breaking records, was engaged by Panhard. He drove an 8.0-litre eight-cylinder sleeve-valve car with a narrow single-seat body at Montlhéry in April and took the World Hour record at 132.01 mph (212.45 km/h).

In May Eyston took the Panhard to Brooklands for the British Empire Trophy where he had a fierce battle with John Cobb who drove the 10.5-litre Delage which had briefly held the Land Speed record in 1924. Cobb won the race but Eyston protested that he had been unable to pass on the tricky Brooklands bankings. After a long hearing, Cobb kept the race. The Delage had been racing with great success at Brooklands where it had held the lap record in 1929 at 132.11 mph (212.56 km/h).

The 4.9-litre Type 54 Bugatti's engine, introduced in 1931, was reputed to have been designed, built and on the road in 13 days using existing parts. It was fast but ill-handling.

PHILIPPE ETANCELIN

Always known affectionately as 'Phi-Phi', Philippe Etancelin was born in Rouen in 1896. His family were wool merchants, a business which always seemed to take priority over his racing. He began competing with a T35 Bugatti in 1926 and won the Marne G. P. at Reims in 1927. Always accompanied by his wife who managed his pit and driving his Bugattis to the circuits, Etancelin began totting up an impressive number of wins, culminating with the 1930 French G. P. at Pau.

In 1931 Etancelin abandoned his Bugattis for an Alfa Romeo. He raced Alfas for three seasons, winning the Le Mans 24-Hour race in 1934, co-driving with Paris-based Italian Luigi Chinetti, and later moved on to a Maserati. He came back to the blue in 1937 with a Talbot-Lago and chased the dominant German teams in Grands Prix in 1938 and 1939, picking up a number of places.

After World War 2 Phi-Phi bought a 26C Talbot and became a regular member of the Grand Prix circus for several seasons, joining the other greying, middle-aged Talbot drivers who so enlivened the racing scene in those years. In 1949 he won the Paris G. P. and came second in the Italian G. P. His last season was 1953. After finishing second at Rouen he was decorated as a Chevalier of the Legion d'Honneur. He died in 1981.

Etancelin was a true motor-racing character, a large cheerful man who was universally popular. His racing style was idiosyncratic. He wore a cloth cap turned back to front and had a distinctive wheel-sawing style of driving. Practising before a race, he would leave the pits and drive round the circuit at

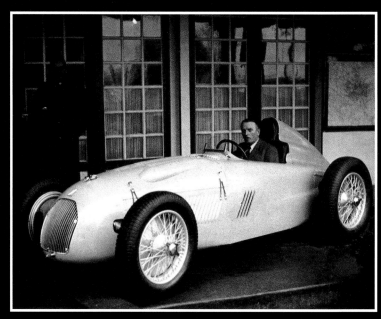

Phi-Phi Etancelin drove the offset 4.5-litre Talbot in the 1939 French Grand Prix.

a slow touring speed for several laps. Gradually he increased the pace until he worked up to full racing speed. He maintained this custom even when he knew the circuit well.

With less drama, some remarkable records had been established at Montlhéry in March and April of 1932. A Citroën C6 with a 1,452 cc engine, called 'La Petite Rosalie' and sponsored by the Yacco oil company, had driven round the banked track almost interminably to set World records for times and distances from 19 to 54 days and 50,000 miles to 130,000 km.

In June of 1932 France mourned Andre Boillot who had been killed in a minor hill climb with a prototype 996 cc 201X Peugeot which had an engine designed by Bugatti. France acknowledged the achievements of Ettore Bugatti when he was appointed an Officer of the Legion d'Honneur in August 1932.

It was realised at Molsheim that the T51 had reached the end of the road and the T54 was not the answer so work began on a new design. Meanwhile Chiron had left the Bugatti team. He had had a poor relationship with team manager Meo Costantini, exacerbated when Costantini made passes at Alice Hoffmann, who was now living with Chiron.

Some comfort came for Bugatti from Italy. Alfa Romeo, suffering a financial crisis, had withdrawn from racing and refused to release its Type Bs to Enzo Ferrari. Ferrari, who now carried the banner for Alfa Romeo, had to run the obsolescent Monzas in 1933. This strange decision meant the T51 was competitive again for the 1933 season.

The first major race was at Monaco. The 100-lap contest was one of the greatest Grand Prix races of all time. Varzi in a T51 was matched against his hated rival Nuvolari in a Monza Alfa. From the start the pair battled, never more than a few lengths apart. Nuvolari led for 66 laps and Varzi for 34 laps. In the closing laps Nuvolari pulled away, but with a huge effort Varzi caught up and on lap 99 they crossed the line together. By over-revving his engine to 7,500 rpm Varzi snatched the lead on the hill up to the Casino. Nuvolari responded, but trying to retake the lead in the Tunnel the Alfa engine burst and Varzi went on to win. Throughout the dramatic race the cars never touched and each gave the other room to pass.

A month later the very fast circuit at Tripoli on the edge of the Libyan desert saw a repeat performance. This time Nuvolari led on the last lap but Varzi squeezed by on the line to win by a mere 0.02 seconds. Bugatti hoped to have the new car, the T59, ready for the French G. P. at

The Type 50 Bugatti ran at Le Mans in 1931 but the team withdrew after disastrous tyre failures. Rost, seen here, crashed when a tyre burst and a spectator was killed in the accident.

Though revolutionary, the four-wheel-drive Type 53 Bugatti only gained success in hill climbs. Chiron and Varzi were at the Klausen climb in 1932.

At the Avusrennen races a week earlier Achille Varzi took the honours with a T54, just ahead of Czaikowski in what may have been an arranged finish. Czaikowski continued his run of success at Brooklands where the T54 ran away with the British Empire Trophy.

The background to Italian racing was always full of high drama. Nuvolari was so angered by the absence of the Type B Alfa Romeos that he stormed out of the Scuderia Ferrari and went to Maserati. This persuaded Alfa Romeo to release the cars to Ferrari so for the rest of the season the Bugatti team was back where it had been in 1932.

At Monza in September the Italian G. P. was supported by a short sprint race, the Monza G. P., with heats and a final. The race was marred when on the opening lap of the second heat Campari in an Alfa, Borzacchini in a Maserati and Czaikowski in his T54 went off the track. All were killed.

The T59 Bugatti, the replacement for the T51, was largely the work of Jean Bugatti. It had appeared in the paddock at Spa but had not raced. It finally made its debut for the Spanish G. P. at San Sebastian, the last big race of 1933. It is regarded as one of the most beautiful racing cars of all time with its superb proportions and its remarkable wheels with radial 'piano wire' spokes. Perhaps retrograde, it had a two-seat body and initially an engine of 2.8 litres. It was a disappointment. It lacked pace and Varzi finished fourth nearly 25 minutes behind the winning Type B Alfa. Worse still, it was beaten by the T51 of private entrant Marcel Lehoux.

In the Grand Prix world the once-dominant power of Bugatti was fading fast. It was a happier story in the fast-growing class of 1,500 cc racing. Here Pierre Veyron, a test driver at Molsheim, was racing a 1.5-litre T51A and was the man to beat, scoring wins throughout the 1933 season. Backing up Veyron's successes, the French blue was also being carried to victory by José Scaron's Type MCO single-seat Amilcar. But everything was about to change, not only in Grand Prix racing but also in the lesser *Voiturette* world.

The 3.3-litre Type 59 Bugatti is regarded as one of the most beautiful Grand Prix cars ever. Sadly it was a racing disappointment when it made its debut in 1933.

Montlhéry at the beginning of June, but it was well behind schedule and as no preparation had been done on the T51s, the team was withdrawn.

Count Stanislaw Czaikowski was a Pole, living in France. Having raced Bugattis for several seasons, he was probably giving some financial support to Ettore Bugatti. Czaikowski had a T54 which he took to the Avus track outside Berlin in May 1933 to break the World hour record. This was a remarkable feat as the Avus was two six-mile (10-km) straights linked by long harpins, so the T54 had to slow to 80 mph (130 km/h) twice on every lap. The new hour figure was 132.87 mph (213.65 km/h).

The Citroën 'La Petite Rosalie 2' ran at
Montlhéry for months, establishing World records.

AMILCAR
PARIS

José Scaron scored many wins with his
1.1-litre MCO Amilcar in 1931 and 1932.
Here he was racing on the sands at La Baule.

The 8.0-litre Panhard-Levassor of George Eyston set a World Hour record at Montlhéry in 1932.

CHAPTER 9

A Faded Blue

AT the beginning of 1934 great political turmoil in France culminated on 6 February when rioting demonstrators tried to storm the Chamber of Deputies in Paris. During a pitched battle between the rioters and the police, 15 were killed and 1,500 were injured. On the same day, while Paris was in a state of virtual war, George Eyston was at Montlhéry with the 8.0-litre Panhard. He raised the World Hour record, previously held by Czaikowski, to 133.01 mph (214.01 km/h). Next day Eyston went to Czaikowski's grave at Houville-la-Branche, near Chartres, to lay a wreath.

While France was in turmoil, so too was the Grand Prix world. A new formula came into force for the 1934 season. It seemed simple: a maximum weight limit of 750 kg, less tyres and liquids, and a minimum body width of 85 cm. What changed everything was the return to Grand Prix racing of Daimler-Benz backed up by the new German team of Auto Union, with both encouragement and support from the Nazi regime.

For the new formula Bugatti enlarged the T59 to 3.3 litres. The drivers had changed. Varzi had waited for the T59, but after the disappointing Spanish debut he went off to Alfa Romeo. Bugatti signed René Dreyfus and a promising newcomer, Jean-Pierre Wimille. Veyron was already on the Molsheim payroll and Robert Benoist, who had been managing a Paris garage since his Championship in 1927, was also signed up. The wealth of racing champions has improved since those days.

The first major race was at Monaco. Nuvolari came with a T59, painted red. He had not made up his differences with Enzo Ferrari or Maserati so needed a car. Tazio made a loose arrangement with Bugatti that he would drive a T59 in selected races during the season. The T59s weighed in below the limit but needed strips added to the body sides to comply with the new formula's width requirements.

In the race Dreyfus was third and Nuvolari fifth behind the Alfas, but the Germans hadn't yet made their debut. In the races which followed it was evident that the T59 was off the pace. In the French G. P. at Montlhéry the German cars appeared and outperformed the rest of the field until stricken with minor mechanical bothers. It was an Alfa win and Benoist was the only T59 finisher in fourth place.

At Spa neither German team turned up as there had been a customs dispute about fuel. This left a straight Alfa-Bugatti fight and the Alfas ran into trouble, which left Dreyfus and the team's newcomer, Italian Antonio Brivio, to come an unexpected first and second with their T59s. Sadly this was the last major Bugatti win in

Grands Prix. After ten glorious years it all would now be downhill.

There seemed to be a faint glimmer of hope at the newly-instituted Swiss Grand Prix over a circuit in the Bremgarten, a park in the suburbs of Bern. Dreyfus battled with Hans Stuck's Auto Unions for the lead after the Mercedes team had troubles, but had to stop for water in the closing laps and came third.

With Bugatti realising that top-level racing was a lost cause, entries of the T59 became infrequent. Nuvolari came back for the Spanish G. P. late in September and used his virtuosity to leave the Auto Unions and Alfa Romeos behind and battle with the Mercedes, finishing third. Veyron was still racing his T51A in 1,500 cc races and scored several wins at the beginning of the season, but both the British MGs and 4CM Maseratis were improving, so by the end of 1934 the T51A, like the T59, was becoming an also-ran.

The SEFAC appeared after World War 2 in its Dommartin incarnation.

The double-four SEFAC engine was an intriguing conceit that failed to function well.

Jean Bugatti, seen here at Shelsley Walsh in 1932, crashed the Type 53 Bugatti.

Pierre Veyron won the 1,500 cc race at the Avus in 1934 with his Type 51A Bugatti.

The Monte Carlo Rally dated from 1911. After a break during the war years it was revived in 1924 and by 1930 becoming appreciated by manufacturers as a means of gaining publicity. Hotchkiss, whose principal trade was in arms manufacture, had begun making cars at St Denis, the Paris suburb, in 1903. Until the late 1920s the Hotchkiss had been a staid sort of car, but in 1929 a higher-performance model, the 2,511 cc AM73, was designed by Vincente Bertarione, who had arrived from Talbot.

Driven by Maurice Vasselle, this new Hotchkiss won the 1932 Monte. He followed up with another win in 1933 with a 3,485 cc Hotchkiss 620. There was a Hotchkiss hat-trick in 1934, when Louis Gas and Trevoux scored again with a 620.

Apart from record breaking and a win in the 1925 Monte, Renault had done little on the motor-sporting front. There had been an atypical entry of three 4.2-litre eight-cylinder Nervastellas for the 1930 Tourist Trophy. These were withdrawn after poor Garfield was killed in a practice accident, but Liocourt was the victor in the 1930 Morocco Rally. There was little activity after that. A special Nervasport saloon broke the 48-hour record at Montlhéry in April 1934, then a Nervasport coupé, with the eight-cylinder engine enlarged to 5,448 cc, won the Monte in 1935 driven by Christian Lahaye and Quartresous.

Although Bugatti was declining in the Grand Prix world, French hopes for a revival rose at the beginning of 1935. With the realisation that new blood was needed, intervention came from the Popular Front government that had come to power after the 1934 riots. Industrial production was flagging and unemployment was a grave problem. Despite these difficulties the Société d'Etude et de Fabrication d'Automobiles de Course or SEFAC was established. This was charged with the construction of a racing car to bring back former glories.

To finance SEFAC, the Comité de la Souscription Nationale pour Fonds de Course was formed with the task of raising funds by public subscription, selling lapel badges and soliciting money from industry. Not much money was forthcoming. Emil Petit, who had been the guiding force behind Salmson in the 1920s, was engaged to design a car.

Petit came up with a 3.0-litre eight-cylinder design composed of two four-cylinder blocks side-by-side. This went into a chassis which, apart from independent front suspension, was a throwback to the 1920s. The SEFAC appeared for the French G. P. at Montlhéry in June of 1935, but Petit had done his sums badly and it weighed 900 kg; so to red faces all round it was taken away unraced, not to be seen again for three years.

Bugatti was promising a new Grand Prix car, so France waited. Meanwhile the Italian Piero Taruffi, who was now a Molsheim works driver, dropped out of the Eifelrennen with a T59 and Wimille gained some wins in minor races. The new car was promised for the French G. P. Cars had to be presented for technical inspection and weighing before the race. The officials waited until almost midnight on the day preceding the race. With minutes to spare the Bugatti appeared, but it was a huge anti-climax as it was a T59 fitted with the old engine from Czaikowski's T54. Rushed through the weighing, it was certainly over the 750 kg limit. In the race it retired when at the back of the field.

It was much the same story for the rest of the 1935 season. In the Belgian G. P. at Spa Wimille held third place amongst the Mercedes for a few laps then dropped out. It was slightly better at San Sebastian where Wimille split the Mercedes team, holding third place for most of the race, only being demoted to fourth just before the finish.

The Type 59 Bugatti was weighed before Dreyfus's win in the 1934 Belgian Grand Prix at Spa. It was Bugatti's last major G. P. victory.

Left: Lucy O'Reilly Schell was highly influential in the Delahaye racing programme.

Nor were French efforts looking better in the *Voiturette* class. Veyron's T51A Bugatti was now completely outclassed by the new British ERAs. He gained one last win in the 1935 Albi G. P.

There was a significant happening at the end of September. The British season finished with the British Racing Drivers' Club 500-Mile Race at Brooklands. This was a flat-out blind around the punishing Brooklands track, an event which only a tough car could survive. Bugatti sent a T59 with the supercharger removed. It was co-piloted by two leading British drivers, Lord Howe and Brian Lewis. Howe had been a great Bugatti supporter for many seasons, racing a T51 and a T59. The car ran rapidly and finished third. It would probably have won the race but for two brief stops by Lewis to deal with an over-pressurised fuel tank.

Delahaye was an engineering company which became one of the early manufacturers in France. The first Delahaye, built at Tours, appeared in 1895 and was followed by a range of worthy but unexciting cars. The company moved to Paris in 1897 where it was joined by Charles Weiffenbach who subsequently took control. Under Weiffenbach production continued into the 1920s with a range of cars and lorries. In 1927 a new overhead-valve six-cylinder lorry engine was introduced.

By the early 1930s Delahaye was coming to a halt, but Weiffenbach—with an imaginative stroke—decided to take the company up-market, producing a range of luxury cars with a sporting image based around a 3.2-litre development of the lorry engine, with transverse-leaf independent front suspension. Albert Perrot, who had raced in the Salmson works team in the 1920s, joined Delahaye as a test and development driver.

Several Delahayes ran in the 1934 Monte Carlo Rally. In May of 1934 a single-seat saloon was taken to Montlhéry where Perrot, Armand Girod and Marcel Dhôme raised the World 48-hour record to 109.47 mph (176.29 km/h). In October 1934 Perrot took a Delahaye to North Africa for the Grand Prix de Tourisme, run on a circuit outside Algiers and came home first.

LOUIS CHIRON

Often known as 'Louis the Debonair', Louis Chiron was born in Monaco in 1899, the son of the maître d'hôtel of the Hotel de Paris. During World War 1 he was the personal driver of Marshal Pètain. After the war he became a professional dance partner at the Hotel de Paris and began driving a T22 Bugatti in local races on the Riviera. He persuaded a rich American woman to buy him a T30 Bugatti and with this became the local champion in 1925.

Chiron's talents were spotted by Alfred Hoffmann, the Hoffmann-La Roche pharmaceutical heir. Hoffmann sponsored Chiron with a T35 Bugatti in 1926 and 1927. Chiron obtained an unexpected additional bonus as Hoffmann's wife Alice became his mistress.

With an enhanced reputation from his successes in Hoffmann's Bugattis, Chiron was recruited into the Bugatti works team and became the virtual number one driver in 1928. He scored a string of wins culminating in the G. P. d'Europe at Monza. He stayed with Bugatti for five seasons, the best of which was 1931, driving the new twin-cam T51, when he won his local Monaco G. P., the French G. P. at Montlhéry and the Czech G. P. at Brno.

Rivalry for Alice's affections forced Chiron's departure from Bugatti. In 1933 he raced an Alfa Romeo in a private team with German Rudi Caracciola. It was a short move to the Scuderia Ferrari, virtually the official Alfa team. With the Scuderia he gained several wins, notably the 1934 French G. P. He was appointed a Chevalier of the Legion d'Honneur at the end of the 1935 season. Chiron joined the Mercedes-Benz team in 1936, but it was an unhappy time with the German cars not at their best. He had several accidents and Alice left him to marry Caracciola.

Louis Chiron announced his retirement at the end of the 1936 season, but Antony Lago persuaded him to join the Talbot team in 1937 and he won the French G. P. again. Then he retired again from the sport. Chiron came out again after World War 2, rejoining Talbot to race the 1939 monoplace. With this he had

Louis Chiron was perhaps seeking divine guidance before the 1947 French Grand Prix.

several minor wins and also took the first post-war French G. P. at Lyon in 1947. In 1949, at the age of 50, Chiron scored his last win with a 26C Talbot taking the French G. P. again at Reims.

Chiron carried on for several seasons racing a Maserati and an Osca in the early years of the F1 World Championship, even in his 50s picking up a handful of championship points. His last race was at Monaco in 1955 driving a D50 Lancia. He tried his hand at rallying and pulled off a win in the 1954 Monte, also with a Lancia. After that he devoted himself to the organisation of the Monaco G. P. He died in 1979.

Always recognised for his style and flair, Louis Chiron was a fine driver considered by some in the early 1930s the best in Europe. His success was aided by an empathy with his cars. He was capable of nursing a sick car to a win when others would have broken it.

A rich American, Laury Schell, whose wife Lucy had raced a Bugatti in the 1920s, commissioned competition cars from Delahaye. During the 1935 season the Schells and Perrot notched up wins in sports-car races at Nancy, Orleans and Reims. In a first appearance at Le Mans, a car driven by 'Michel Paris' and Marcel Mongin finished fifth. The Delahaye was still an ungainly high-built car, but in the autumn of 1935 a new model, the 135, was introduced. This was lower with an enlarged 3.6-litre engine and a short-chassis competition model was offered.

This new Delahaye and France's other sporting marques received a stimulus in 1936. Realising that in Grand Prix racing Bugatti and SEFAC were a busted flush, the ACF decided that there was little point in holding the French Grand Prix as a showcase for the rising might of Germany. It announced that in 1936 the French G. P. would be a sports-car race. Other clubs organising races in France were encouraged to follow the lead of the ACF and promote races for sports cars .

This decision was welcomed enthusiastically by French manufacturers and the French racing world. Delahaye, Talbot and Bugatti had suitable cars to ensure a high level of competition. The stage was set for a French Racing Blue renaissance.

The Delahaye took the World 48-Hour and 10,000 km records at Montlhéry in May of 1934.

The Renault Nervasport set records at Montlhéry in April of 1934.

The first Delahaye appearance at Le Mans was by the high-chassis Type 135 which took fifth place in 1935, driven by 'Paris' and Mongin.

The Type 57 Bugatti of Brian Lewis led the similar car of Lord Howe in the 1935 Ulster Tourist Trophy in Ireland.

The Blue Renaissance

The Delahaye Type 135 played a big part in reviving the fortunes of French blue.

THERE was to be another major player in the sports-car racing arena created in 1936 by the ACF. The Sunbeam-Talbot-Darracq combine had run into financial difficulties brought about by the burden of loans taken in the early 1920s to meet the cost of its racing activities, largely based around Sunbeam. When the guaranteed notes covering those loans matured in 1934 there was no money in the STD kitty. The group was broken up and its component parts sold off.

Managing the French component of Talbot-Darracq at Suresnes was a Franco-Italian, Anthony Lago. Lago found backers who put up the funds to make him the owner of Talbot-Darracq. Like Delahaye, the Talbot-Darracq range had been stodgy, but Lago engaged Walter Becchia, who had been a key designer with Fiat in the 1920s. Becchia reworked an existing 3.0-litre six cylinder engine, fitting a pushrod-and-rocker cylinder head which gave a hemispherical combustion chamber. This engine went into a low chassis which became the Talbot T150. At the beginning of 1936 the engine was enlarged to 4.0 litres and the sports-racing T150C appeared.

The first major event of the 1936 season was the Monaco G. P. Bugatti, still hankering after Grand Prix glory, entered a T59 converted to a single-seater, or *monoplace*, which became known as the T59/50B. It was withdrawn after practice. In the race two normal T59s driven by Wimille and 'Williams' were completely outclassed.

The French sports-car season began at the featureless Miramas track with a three-hour race which saw the debut of the new Delahayes and Talbots. The Delahayes took the first six places with 'Paris' as the winner after the three Talbots dropped out.

France was crippled by industrial unrest in the spring and summer of 1936. Ettore Bugatti, who had run his Molsheim factory as a paternal autocracy, was horrified when his workers joined the strikers. He retired to Paris deeply hurt and left the Molsheim management to son

80

Jean. An immediate result of the strikes was the cancellation of the Le Mans 24 Hours. Despite the industrial inaction the Bugatti racing department remained working.

A new touring Bugatti, the T57 with a 3.3-litre twin-cam eight-cylinder engine, had appeared in 1934. Owing much to the design of the T59, it was largely the work of Jean Bugatti. A highly tuned and much-modified T57 was built for the French G. P. Called the T57G, it had an all-enveloping body which was a foretaste of the designs of the 1950s. Three T57Gs were entered for the French G. P. at Montlhéry. It was a 1,000-km race so the driving was shared.

The Bugattis were the fastest cars in the field and left the Delahayes and Talbots behind. At 300 km the T57Gs held the first three places, but were delayed by the need to change brake shoes. At the finish the Bugatti of Wimille and

Raymond Sommer was the winner in front of five Delahayes led by the car of 'Paris' and Mongin. The other T57Gs were held back by the braking problems and finished in sixth and 13th places. Bugatti was just about back on top, albeit in a different sphere, so the ACF felt the change of emphasis had been fully justified.

The action moved to Reims for the 1936 Marne G. P. Here the Talbots were getting into their stride, René Dreyfus taking his into the lead and pulling away from the T57Gs until the crankshaft broke. He then took over the Talbot of 'Heldé' and chased after the lead again, but Wimille's Bugatti was too far ahead and won. The T57G of Benoist was second and the Talbot third. The Delahayes had been outpaced.

Though the Spa 24 Hours was greatly increased in importance with the Le Mans cancellation, Bugatti gave it

The three big French players: a Bugatti Type 57G led a Type 150 Talbot and a Type 135 Delahaye during the 1936 French Grand Prix at Montlhéry.

A Talbot Type 150.

by a crash in which Marcel Lehoux, who had been a successful Bugatti driver since the mid-1920s, was killed.

The AC du Midi, which promoted the Comminges Grand Prix, jumped on the sports-car bandwagon for their race on 9 August. The regulations permitted sports cars to run stripped so Bugatti, much to the annoyance of other entrants, entered two full Grand Prix T59s fitted with the unblown T57G engine. There was talk of a boycott, but the race went ahead and Wimille ran away with it, followed home by two Talbots.

The T59/50B was run in the Swiss Grand Prix at Berne, perhaps to show the Fonds de Course that Bugatti was still serious about racing in the top echelon, but it was completely outclassed and lasted only three laps. At the end of September the T59/50B was taken across the Atlantic to New York for the Vanderbilt Cup, run over an artificial road circuit at Westbury on Long Island, about 40 miles (60 km) east of New York. The Mercedes and Auto Union teams were absent so Wimille took a very profitable second place behind Nuvolari's 8C 35 Alfa Romeo.

The 750 kg Grand Prix formula should have ended in 1936 but the AIACR decided that it should continue for the 1937 season. It was agreed that a new formula should come into force in 1938. In broad terms this was for

a miss, sending a T59 to the minor Deauville Grand Prix a week later. This was a formula Grand Prix, a rarity in France during 1936. In front of the fashionable holiday crowd Wimille had an easy win though the race was marred

The Type 150 Talbot which won the 1937 French Grand Prix and the 1937 Tourist Trophy stayed in England and was a dominant force in British racing for over ten years—but for legal reasons was called a Darracq.

1937 Type 57G Bugatti

After more than a decade of British and Italian successes in the legendary Le Mans 24-Hour race, the 3.3-litre Type 57G Bugatti restored French pride with its 1937 victory, driven by Jean-Pierre Wimille and Robert Benoist.

The sports-equipped Type 59 Bugatti 'Grand-Mère' had a most successful 1937 season driven by Jean-Pierre Wimille.

that Grands Prix performances had leapt ahead by much more than two per cent since 1934.

It was soon evident that only Bugatti and Delahaye were likely to compete for the prize. Ettore Bugatti, showing considerable guile, approached the Fonds and explained that he wanted to compete for the prize and build a new car but needed funds to take part. The Fonds committee agreed that there would be a subsidiary competition with a prize of 400,000 francs. This would be run under the same conditions as the main prize, but had to be completed by 31 March 1937.

The committee also agreed that a car could run with a capacity 10 per cent larger than that allowed by the new formula, thus making a 3.3-litre T59 Bugatti eligible for the minor prize. If an oversize-engined car won, 20 per cent of the prize would be withheld until a new car came to the line for the 1938 French G. P. Delahaye could not be ready by 31 March and Anthony Lago commented acerbically that the Fonds should just give the 400,000 francs to Bugatti and not bother to run the competition!

The French G. P. was announced as a sports-car race again in 1937 as were most other races in France. Encouraged by the success at Comminges the previous year, a T59 Bugatti was prepared for the 1937 season, fitted with a T57G engine and a sleek sports body. To keep race organisers happy and perhaps to placate the opposition, it was given a T57 chassis number.

The season opened in February at Pau where Wimille's disguised T59 walked away with the race. After Pau the car went back to Molsheim where it was converted back to a full supercharged Grand Prix T59. In this form it went to Montlhéry for the 400,000 franc competition. It was a disaster. First it rained, preventing Wimille from achieving the average speed. Then the fuel pump broke and when that was repaired the back axle failed.

Time had run out and the deadline of 31 March had come. Ettore Bugatti pleaded with the Fonds committee which, after obtaining the consent of Charles Weiffenbach

supercharged 3.0-litre cars and unsupercharged 4.5-litre cars. A sliding scale of weights was intended to give parity to smaller-engined cars, but it soon became evident that the subsidiary weight provisions were impracticable. For the French manufacturers the new formula had possibilities as their sports cars, running stripped and more highly tuned, could be elevated to the Grand Prix ranks.

The coffers of the Fonds de Course had been filling rapidly during 1936 because the French government had imposed a levy on driving-licence fees which went to the Fonds. In January 1937 it was announced that there would be a competition amongst French manufacturers, the winner of which would get most of the accumulated funds to assist in building a car for the new 1938 Grand Prix formula.

One million francs would go to the manufacturer whose new car exceeded by the greatest margin an average speed of 146.51 km/h (90.98 mph) over 200 km at Montlhéry before 31 August 1937. The target was set by adding two per cent to the average speed recorded by Chiron's Alfa Romeo when winning the 1934 French G. P. over the same course. The Fonds committee seemed to have overlooked of Delahaye and Anthony Lago, extended the deadline to 18 April. Wimille was back at Montlhéry on 12 April. This time the 200-km run was completed inside the time limit by the wafer-thin margin of 4.9 seconds.

Converted back to a sports car, the T59 went to Tunis in May for the local G. P. It was run in three heats, each of 100 km with no refuelling allowed. It became a battle between the Bugatti and Sommer's T150C Talbot. The T59 ran out of fuel on the last lap of the third heat, giving victory to Sommer. The Tunis competitors went on to Bone in Algeria where there was a three-cornered fight amongst the Bugatti, the Delahayes and Talbots. Despite oiled sparking plugs, Wimille won the first heat and came second in the second heat to win on aggregate from the Talbot of Carrière.

The next encampment for the French sports-car circus was at Miramas. This race was also in three heats with refuelling not allowed between heats but permissible during the race. There were two artificial chicanes in the first heat, one in the second and none in the third. Wimille's Bugatti was faster than the Talbots in the first heat but as the course was made faster in the second and third heats, it fell back and then retired, leaving victory to the T150C Talbots of Sommer and Comotti.

Le Mans was back in the calendar on 19 and 20 June of 1937. Bugatti entered two of the T57Gs which had run in the 1936 French G. P. These were matched against seven Type 135 Delahayes, two T150C Talbots and a potent 2900B Alfa Romeo. The Alfa led at the start, then Wimille's T57G went into the lead. In a six-car crash after eight laps two drivers were killed. Soon afterward the Alfa retired and the Bugatti which Wimille was sharing with Robert Benoist sailed on, dominating the race.

There was a moment of anxiety at noon on the Sunday when Benoist went off the road as the brakes began to weaken. After a 10-minute delay the Bugatti was pushed back on to the track without any penalty as it was deemed to be in a dangerous position. Doubtless, a fortuitous decision by the marshals! At the end of the 24 hours it came home to a tumultuous reception, winning by a margin of seven laps from the Delahaye of Joseph Paul and Marcel Mongin and the Delahaye of René Dreyfus and Henri Stoffel.

Finishing in seventh, eighth and tenth places at Le Mans were three 2.0-litre Peugeot 302s. These were an elegant sports-bodied version of the standard 302, entered by Emile Darl'mat, a Paris agent for Peugeot. France was right back on the motor racing map.

Louis Chiron's star had waned after his halcyon years of the early 1930s. His relationship with Alice Hoffmann

had broken up when she left him to marry Rudolf Caracciola. After a lean year with Alfa Romeo in 1935 he joined Mercedes-Benz in 1936, but the results were dismal and he was hurt in a crash in the German G. P. Unhappy and dispirited, he decided to retire from the sport.

Anthony Lago recognised a talent going to waste, so persuaded Chiron to join the Talbot team. After a brief run at Le Mans, terminated when he was involved in the multiple crash, Chiron led the Talbot team in the 310-mile (500-km) 1937 French G. P. at Montlhéry. Bugatti appeared with a T57 fitted with a 4.5-litre development of

René Dreyfus in the Type 145 Delahaye secured the 'Million' prize.

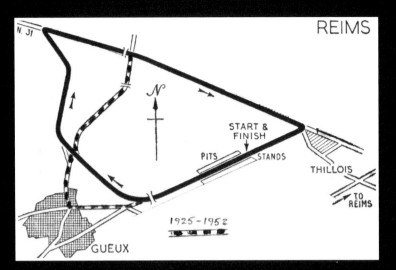

REIMS

1925-1952

GUEUX

REIMS

Reims was one of the great classic Grand Prix road circuits. Racing began there in 1925 when the countryside of the Champagne region was still recovering from the ravages of World War 1. The poplars which lined the roads were still small saplings. The 4.8-mile (7.8-km) circuit to the west of the city of Reims was triangular with two main straights linked by a slightly winding back leg. The fastest leg of the course was the RN31 Reims-Soissons road which joined the grandstand straight at the tight Thillois hairpin. At the end of the grandstand straight a right-angle corner in the village of Gueux led to the winding back leg.

Initially Reims was the home of the Marne G. P., a small local event which grew rapidly until by the end of the 1920s it was a major race on the French calendar. As the race grew in stature the circuit was improved and the roads were widened. Even from its earliest days Reims was recognised as one of the fastest events where high lap speeds were set.

In 1932 Reims was the venue of the French G. P. The race came back again in 1938 and 1939 after the Marne G. P. had been held in the interim years. The French G. P. returned in 1948 and after that Reims was its home until 1956. As well as the G. P. there was a supporting 12-hour sports-car race which began at the unusual hour of midnight.

In 1953 Reims underwent major reconstruction. A new leg was built with an ultra-fast curve after the pits which went on to join the RN31 beyond the former junction with the back leg. This cut out the old back leg and Gueux village. The lap distance was increased to 5.2 miles (8.3 km). The changes made Reims the fastest road circuit in Europe. The nature of the circuit often involved slipstreaming battles and close finishes.

The French G. P. stayed there until 1966, interrupted by occasional departures to Rouen. There were minor races on the circuit until 1970 after which it was abandoned, partly because closing major roads caused too much interruption to local life. Parts of it including the grandstand and pits remained. The legendary organiser of the Reims events was 'Toto' Roche, whose comic antics with a collection of flags enlivened races for many years.

---

the T50 engine but it was withdrawn as unraceworthy. In the opening laps Chiron had a battle with Sommer, also in a Talbot, then Chiron gradually pulled away to a comfortable win with a two-minute margin. Sommer dropped back and Comotti's Talbot came second. Divo completed a Talbot 1-2-3 with the Delahayes unable to match the pace of the Talbots.

Laury and Lucy Schell threw their considerable fortune into backing Delahaye. They formed an aptly named Ecurie Bleue, which effectively became the works team, and funded the design and development of a 4.5-litre V-12 engine. It was the work of Jean Francois, intended to be a dual-purpose unit suitable both for a Delahaye to race under the new Grand Prix formula and for a sports car to replace the Type 135.

The first V-12 Delahaye, the Type 145, appeared at the French G. P. driven by René Dreyfus, but only lasted for eight laps when an oil pump broke. Two Type 145s came to Reims for the Marne G. P. Bugatti had brought out the

sports T59, known affectionately by the Molsheim mechanics as 'Grand-Mère'. Granny lifted her skirts and went. Wimille and the T59 were uncatchable. Dreyfus pursued in the T145 Delahaye until a tyre burst and he went off the road. Carrière's T145 had the same fate and Wimille finished nearly three minutes in front of the Talbots.

The sudden improvement in the performance of the T59 was attributed by rival teams to a mixture of illegal fuel, but with the usual deferential reverence shown to Bugatti when applying regulations the organisers did not investigate the allegations.

Attention in France now returned to the 'Million Franc' competition. It was a straight fight between Bugatti and Delahaye, both of which had to make their runs at Montlhéry before 31 August 1937. Bugatti fitted the 4.5-litre T50 engine into the *monoplace* T59 while Delahaye was relying on a stripped T145 sports car. Bugatti booked the track for an attempt on 15 August, but Wimille was hurt in a road accident. Robert Benoist was briefed to drive the Bugatti on 23 August but was not up to the required pace, so the Bugatti team waited and hoped Wimille would be fit.

Meanwhile the Delahaye had appeared, but broke its gearbox. On 27 August Dreyfus made an attempt with the Delahaye and completed the 200 km just inside the limit by a mere 4.9 seconds. It was now up to Bugatti to reply. On 30 August a still unfit Wimille took the T59 round the track, but the engine lost oil pressure and the gearbox broke. The car was rushed to Bugatti's Paris depot for repairs.

Late in the afternoon of 31 August the T59 was back at Montlhéry where Wimille began an attempt but pulled off after a few laps with a broken half shaft. The Bugatti mechanics tore the axle to pieces and replaced the shaft. At 6:42 p.m. Wimille restarted. He was joined by Dreyfus in the Delahaye, running as a precaution in case Wimille improved on the Delahaye time. The T59 oiled up its plugs and Wimille stopped. At 7:00 p.m., with

new plugs and the light fading, he was back on the track. It was soon all over. The Bugatti began to smoke, then a piston failed. Delahaye had secured the 'Million Francs' prize.

The 'Million Francs' competition marked the end of 1937's French racing season. Three T150C Talbots went to England at the beginning of September for the RAC Tourist Trophy at Donington Park. To avoid trademark conflicts with the English Talbot, the trio were labelled Darracqs. A 12-hour sports-car race at Donington in June 1937 had seen a Type 135 Delahaye victory, the winning car driven by the Siamese driver Prince Bira, who raced with a British licence.

The Tourist Trophy, like almost every major British race in the 1930s, was run as a handicap, but the Darracqs were the fastest cars in the field. Comotti won and Le Begue was second. The winning car remained in England where it became a major force in racing until the early 1950s.

The Darl'mat 302 Peugeot which won the 2.0-litre class at Le Mans in 1937, being exhibited at the Paris Salon.

CHAPTER 11

Frustrations, Triumphs and a Tragedy

THE dawn of the new Grand Prix formula in 1938 marked a lessening of French enthusiasm for sports-car racing. This was understandable as it seemed that Bugatti, Delahaye and Talbot would all become immersed in Grand Prix racing under the new formula. Bugatti announced that there would be a new car. Delahaye proposed to field the sports T145, stripped of road equipment, but announced plans for a *monoplace* funded by the Schell family. At Talbot, Lago commissioned Walter Becchia to work on an ambitious supercharged 3.0-litre V-16 design and the T150C engine was enlarged to 4.5 litres.

The first G. P. race of the 1938 season was at Pau in April. A week earlier Dreyfus had a preliminary canter, running the 'Million Franc' Type 145 Delahaye, now road-equipped, in the

The Type 145 Delahaye had a 4.5-litre V-12.

legendary Mille Miglia, 1,000 testing miles around Italy. Despite many stops to add water to a leaking radiator, he placed fourth against the supercharged 2900B Alfa Romeos.

Mercedes-Benz sent two of their new W154s to Pau, one of which raced. The German car took the lead on the short, tight, street circuit, followed by Dreyfus's Type 145 Delahaye. Dreyfus passed the Mercedes and held the lead for a few laps. The Delahaye with relatively economic fuel consumption ran non-stop and when the Mercedes made refuelling stops it took the lead again. Dreyfus pulled too far ahead to be caught and to French jubilation came home the winner. It seemed that the 'Million Franc' competition had been justified and achieved the hoped-for result.

At the end of April the second formula race was held, unusually in Ireland on the very fast Carrigohane circuit outside Cork. Neither German team was there, but Wimille appeared in a T59/50 Bugatti, now with a 3.0-litre engine. It was not the completely new car that had been expected. Dreyfus was also present with his Type 145 Delahaye.

Dreyfus took the lead on the second lap and ran on to win unchallenged. The Bugatti ran as high as third but was lapped by Dreyfus, then retired with a broken piston. French hopes were still high. The serious season began in May at Tripoli, where on the ultra-fast circuit the Delahaye

Wimille piloted his Type 59/50B Bugatti during the 1938 Cork Grand Prix.

was out-paced. Seventh was the best that Dreyfus could do.

The 1938 Le Mans 24-Hour race lacked a Bugatti entry so it was a battle between two Ecurie Bleue Type 145 Delahayes and a batch of Type 135s, matched against six Talbots and a solitary 2900B Alfa Romeo. The Alfa went into an immediate lead and both Type 145s broke down. The quickest Talbot pursued the Alfa and held the lead for a while, then broke as well.

Early on the Sunday afternoon, with victory almost in sight, the Alfa had a lead of 12 laps. Then it burst a tyre and shortly afterwards stopped with a broken valve. This left the Type 135 Delahaye of Eugène Chaboud and Jean Tremoulet with a comfortable lead over the similar car of Gaston Serraud and Yves Giraud-Cabantous. The Delahayes finished first and second, followed by a T150C Talbot coupé. To round off a satisfactory French weekend a Darl'Mat 402 Peugeot won the 2.0-litre class.

The Fonds de Course was still accruing from the driving-licence levy, so the Committee decided that a further million francs should be disbursed to the team which showed evidence that it was working on a new design for a Grand Prix car. Weiffenbach and the Schells confidently expected that the new V-12 *monoplace* Delahaye, the Type 155, would scoop the pool so were dismayed and angered when the Committee preferred the V-16 Talbot, even though this was still on the drawing board, unlike the Type 155 which was half-built. It was significant that Bugatti was not considered for a grant.

The new formula had not stimulated G. P. racing as expected. After Tripoli there was a gap of almost two months until the French Grand Prix. This was restored to its former glory as a full G. P. and was held on the fast triangular Reims circuit. To show their disgust at the Committee's decision the Schells withdrew the Ecurie Bleue Delahaye entries, which left two stripped T150C sports Talbots to face the Mercedes-Benz and Auto Union teams. Bugatti had to appear to collect the outstanding 20 per cent of the earlier Fonds competition prize.

Late in the afternoon before the race, after practice was finished, the 3.0-litre T59/50 was produced. Wimille started from the back of the grid and was involved in a collision with Rudi Hasse's Auto Union on the first lap. The slightly bent Bugatti limped back to the pits and retired. It was a real 'starting money special', but Bugatti had the cash.

Also on the grid, reappearing after three years in hiding, was the SEFAC, driven by Le Mans winner Chaboud. It did marginally better than the Bugatti, retiring after two slow laps. The two Talbots ran steadily at the back of the field. One finished, ten laps behind the winning Mercedes.

A week after the French G. P. the Spa 24 Hours was held in miserable conditions. The race was won by a 2900B Alfa Romeo, but it was pursued all the way by a 3.0-litre D6-70 Delage which was only one lap behind at the end. It was driven by Louis Gérard, the proprietor of an amusement arcade and cycle track in Paris, and Georges Monneret.

After its glory years of the 1920s Delage had fallen on hard times. In 1935 it was acquired by Walter Watney, the Paris agent of the marque. Watney found there were production problems and did a deal with Charles Weiffenbach for Delahaye to produce a range of Delages made mainly from Delahaye components in the Delahaye factory. A handful of the production D6-70s appeared with sports-racing bodywork.

The Type 145 Delahayes were back for the German G. P. where Dreyfus was fifth, profiting from mechanical problems with the German teams. The Grand Prix circus moved to Italy for the races at Livorno and Pescara, where the *monoplace* Type 155 Delahaye appeared. Its performance was little improvement on the Type 145 and it retired in both races. It was the same sorry tale for the remaining races of the season.

Louis Gérard took his D6-70 Delage to England on 3 September for the Tourist Trophy at Donington. Once

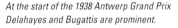

At the start of the 1938 Antwerp Grand Prix Delahayes and Bugattis are prominent.

again it was a handicap race in which Gérard, using the pace of the Delage combined with the useful handicap advantage of its engine size, pulled off an impressive win. The works T150C Talbots, again masquerading as Darracqs, came third and fourth driven by 'Phi-Phi' Etancelin and Carrière.

Apart from the Delage win in England, by the end of 1938 French blue seemed to be fading again. René Dreyfus summed it up in his autobiography *My Two Lives*: 'The season was ending dismally. Reality can be rude. Delahaye was falling apart. Bugatti was fading. Talbot's star had stopped rising. In international motor sport, France was sad.'

Despite its hopes for 'peace for our time', the Munich Agreement in September 1938 was the warning for Europe of an impending war. France began to re-arm and all the motor manufacturers received arms contracts. At the beginning of 1939 Ecurie Bleue continued to work on the central-seated Type 155 Delahaye while the Delahaye factory began to make lorries for the French Army. Bugatti, now in considerable financial trouble and waiting for money to come from promised arms contracts, had abandoned the Grand Prix world but planned to return to Le Mans.

The most ambitious plans were being hatched at the small Talbot works at Suresnes. Three cars were laid down, two as offset *monoplaces* to take the unblown 4.5-litre engine and the third a pure *monoplace*, designed for the supercharged V-16.

The 1939 Grand Prix season began at Pau. The Ecurie Bleue Delahayes were withdrawn so Etancelin carried the blue with one of the new offset Talbots. Running steadily he finished third, two laps behind the winning Mercedes. The SEFAC came out again, and this time—to universal amazement—it lasted for 35 laps, driven by Jean Tremoulet.

A sports Bugatti built up from T59/50B bits was taken to a race in Luxembourg by Wimille, where it beat an impressive entry of works Alfa Romeos. Two weeks later Wimille was at Le Mans with Veyron to drive a T57C. This was a blown version of the normal T57 touring car and had a body similar to, but an improvment upon, the 1937 winner. In the race the Bugatti pair bided their time while the lead was contested by various Talbots, Delahayes and the Gérard/Monneret Delage. By 4:00 a.m. on the Sunday morning the Bugatti was running second to the Delage but had to make a long stop to replace a wheel which was breaking up. This dropped it back to sixth.

Though the brilliant Wimille put on the pace he was still three laps behind at noon, when the Delage began to

misfire. It stopped for several plug changes which let the Bugatti into the lead. It stayed there to win the race amid scenes of great jubilation. The misfiring Delage was second. It was the last major victory for Bugatti; the end of the road was nigh.

A week later, in a tragic Belgian G. P. where Dick Seaman crashed fatally while leading the race, the completely outclassed Type 135 Delahayes of Robert Mazaud and Gèrard came fourth and fifth, profiting from many accidents in the wet conditions. The V-16 Talbot engine was never completed and the *monoplace* appeared at Reims for the French G. P. with a 4.5-litre unblown engine instead. The neat, sleek car was entrusted to the British driver Raymond Mays, who had been the co-founder of ERA and would be the driving force behind BRM in the post-war years. Mays only had a brief race as the Talbot's fuel tank split after ten laps. After the entire Mercedes team dropped out, Lebegue and Etancelin finished in third and fourth places with the offset cars behind a pair of Auto Unions.

At the Nürburgring for the German G. P. the Type 155 *monoplace* Delahaye was brought out again, but after bothers in practice Dreyfus drove a Type 145 in the race. When the Mercedes and Auto Unions either crashed or broke down he was able to work up to fourth place at the finish, albeit two laps or 28 miles (45 km) behind the winner. The Schells had realised that Delahaye was a lost cause so in the Swiss G. P., late in August, Ecurie Bleue entered a pair of new Maseratis.

Jean Bugatti had agreed to run the Le Mans-winning car in a minor meeting at La Baule. On the evening of 11 August while testing the car on the road near the Bugatti factory he swerved to avoid a cyclist in the dusk. The car went off the road and hit a tree. Jean Bugatti was killed instantly. It was a shattering blow for Ettore Bugatti, even more so as Jean had become the driving force in the company.

Bugatti was already in grave financial difficulties. There had been plans to move car production to Belgium to avoid creditors, but before these could be implemented the German army invaded Poland on 1 September. Two days later France was at war.

Dreyfus competed in the unsuccessful Type 155 Delahaye in the 1938 Donington Grand Prix.

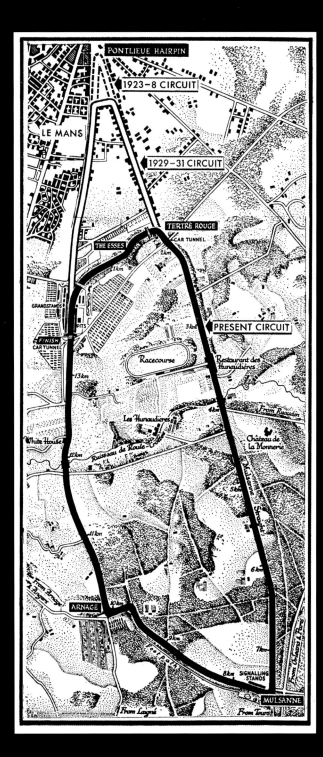

Le Mans

Le Mans in France's Sarthe region has been a vital centre of French motor racing since the earliest days. It was the scene of the first French Grand Prix in 1906, run on a 64-mile (103-km) circuit west of the city. In 1921 it was the venue of the first French Grand Prix after World War 1. The rough stony 10.7-mile (17-km) circuit used in 1921 nurtured the start of a legend two years later when the first 24-hour race was run over it. Le Vingt-Quatre Heures was a magnet for every French manufacturer that had ambitions of glory. Many reputations were made and broken there in the early years.

Gradually the circuit was refined and shortened. Originally it ran into the outskirts of the city but this section was lopped off in 1929. Another change in 1933 was the building of a new section. This reduced the circuit approximately to its present length of 8.3 miles (13.4 km). Permanent pits and grandstands were built in the 1930s.

The circuit suffered extensive damage during World War 2 and did not re-open until 1949. The terrible disaster in the 1955 race when 81 spectators were killed resulted in the widening of the pits straight and the building of a new pits complex. A short version, the Bugatti circuit, was built in the infield during the 1960s. This used the main pits and was the venue for the 1967 French Grand Prix.

The ever-increasing speeds of cars in the 24-hour race forced further changes in the Le Mans layout. In the 1970s artificial bends were built in the notorious White House section to slow cars approaching the pits straight. By 1990 cars were achieving 250 mph (400 km/h) on the Mulsanne Straight, so chicanes were introduced to reduce the speeds.

The many changes and alterations left virtually nothing of the original circuit of the 1920s. Despite this the Circuit Permanente de la Sarthe is among the most evocative circuits in the world and the home of the most famous race of all. It continues to be an irresistible magnet for manufacturers and racing enthusiasts alike.

In 1953, Briggs Cunningham's fourth year at Le Mans, his C5R jumped into the lead from the start ahead of a Talbot-Lago, other Cunninghams and an Allard and Lancia.

This Type 57C Bugatti won at Le Mans in 1939. A few weeks later Jean Bugatti was killed testing this car.

Gianfranco Comotti used opposite lock with his Type 145 Delahaye during the 1938 Mille Miglia.

Amédée Gordini built this 1939 Simca-based 1.1-litre car.

Dreyfus rounded the Thillois Hairpin at Reims in the 1939 French Grand Prix with the Type 145 Delahaye.

The D6-70 Delage nearly defeated the Bugatti at Le Mans in 1939. Driven by Gerard and Monneret, it came second.

CHAPTER 12

Darkness then Sunshine

WHEN France went to war in September 1939 many of her racing drivers were called to the colours. France had maintained compulsory military service between the wars and so most Frenchmen were on the army reserve. French racing-car manufacturers went over to arms production.

The Bugatti factory at Molsheim was considered to be particularly vulnerable to attack with its proximity to the German border, so during the autumn of 1939 the factory was stripped and all its machine tools were moved to Bordeaux. By February 1940 crankshafts for Hispano-Suiza aero engines were being machined in the temporary Bordeaux workshops. In Paris the Delahaye factory turned all its production over to army lorries.

After the first months of the war which were relatively tranquil, the nightmare for France began when the German army invaded Holland and Belgium in May 1940, then broke through the French army and swept across France. On 22 June a defeated France signed an armistice and the German occupation began. The German occupiers ordered Ettore Bugatti to move all his plant back to Molsheim, but to forestall this Bugatti dismissed all his staff.

Alsace had been taken from France and incorporated into the German Reich as a condition of the armistice and the Molsheim factory was compulsorily purchased. Production of military amphibious vehicles began there in 1941, followed later by torpedo motor parts and components of V-1 flying bombs. Ettore Bugatti moved permanently to Paris, where he had been based for some years, and with a nucleus of staff began designs intended for production when the war ended.

Although ordered to produce trucks for the German army, mysteriously Delahaye's production dwindled to nothing. Charles Weiffenbach managed to find countless excuses for the production failures. Virtually no trucks came from the factory during the German occupation.

Jean-Pierre Wimille, Robert Benoist and Pierre Veyron were reservists and rejoined the army. 'Williams' returned to England and enlisted in the British Army. When France fell in 1940 Wimille and Benoist returned to Paris where in May 1942 they were joined by 'Williams', now Captain William Grover-Williams. 'Williams' organised a Resistance circuit, recruiting Wimille and Benoist as aides. The group was notably effective and carried out some successful sabotage operations.

In August 1943 'Williams' was captured. He was taken to Fresnes prison and then to Gestapo headquarters in Berlin where, despite prolonged torture, he gave nothing away. He was executed at Sachsenhausen concentration

camp in March 1945. After 'Williams' was arrested command of his group was taken over by Benoist. He was captured and escaped. Captured again in June 1944 Benoist, like 'Williams', despite torture gave nothing away. He was hanged at Buchenwald concentration camp in September 1944. Wimille and Veyron evaded capture until France was liberated in 1944 and Veyron was awarded the Croix de Guerre for his work in the Resistance.

The war in Europe finished in May 1945. After detonation of the first atomic bombs in August 1945 Japan surrendered and World War 2 was over. Remarkably, just over three weeks after the Japanese surrender a motor-racing meeting was held in the Bois de Boulogne in Paris on a 1.7-mile (2.7-km) circuit. Though a minor event it had great symbolic significance.

Appearing with the *monoplace* 4.7-litre T59/50B Bugatti, Wimille was supported by Ettore Bugatti himself who had entered the car and arrived in one of the enormous and legendary Bugatti Royales. Wimille's principal opponent in the main race, the 43-lap Coupe des Prisonniers, was the 1939 *monoplace* Talbot driven by

Raymond Sommer. The Talbot led for four laps then Wimille went by and swept on to victory.

It seemed that all was well again. Bugatti seemed to have shaken off the terrible traumas following Jean's death. It was announced in October 1945 that a production line of a new racing Bugatti, the T73C, was being laid down. Sadly nothing came of it. A few parts were made, but Ettore Bugatti was more concerned to have the Molsheim factory restored to him. His claims, which were opposed by the communist trade unions, were heard by several courts and the proceedings were drawn out until the spring of 1947.

While awaiting the courts' decision Bugatti had a stroke in May 1947 and died the following August, aged 65. It seemed the end of the road for the Bugatti marque. With the death of Jean, followed by that of Ettore, there seemed no one to carry on the intensely personal family business. A great and glorious chapter in the history of French Racing Blue appeared to have closed. However young Roland Bugatti and the factory's director Pierre Marco would have other ideas.

At the start of the Coupe des Prisonniers, the main event at the first post-war race meeting held in the Bois de Boulogne in September 1945, Levegh's Talbot Type 150 had a narrow lead.

Wimille was the winner of the Coupe des Prisonniers in his Type 59/50B Bugatti.

The FIA (Federation Internationale de l'Automobile), which had succeeded the AIACR as the governing body of motor racing, announced that a new Grand Prix formula, commencing in 1947, would be for 1.5-litre supercharged cars and 4.5-litre unsupercharged machines. This seemed an ideal formula for Delahaye and Talbot whose unblown single-seaters, supported by stripped sports cars, would give France front-rank contenders.

In 1946 a makeshift season of races in France and Italy ran largely to *formule libre*, though by the end of the season some organisers were anticipating the new formula. Unfortunately it soon became evident that while there was less of a gap between the 4.5-litre unblown cars and the 1.5-litre blown cars than there had been with the 3.0-litre blown cars of 1938-39, the supercharged cars were still quicker. The Talbots and Delahayes were almost a match for the obsolete British ERAs and the earlier 6CM Maseratis, but the newer 4CL Maseratis were

ahead and the Type 158 Alfa Romeos were in a different league.

The only driver who offered a challenge to the blown cars was Louis Chiron at the wheel of the 1939 *monoplace* Talbot, prepared at the Suresnes works and entered by Ecurie France. He picked up two second places in the Paris suburbs with races at St Cloud and in the Bois de Boulogne. In September 1946 the G. P. del Valentino, in a Turin park, was in effect the Italian G. P. and was run to the new formula. In a full Italian field dominated by the Type 158 Alfas, Eugene Chaboud managed to take fourth place in a stripped 135 Delahaye.

At the end of the season the G. P. du Salon, again in the Bois de Boulogne, was also run to the new formula. While battling for the lead Chiron had a lucky escape when he hit a stray dog which did a lot of damage to the front of his Talbot. Levegh took third place in a stripped T150C Talbot behind two Maseratis.

Surprisingly in an austerity-hit post-war Europe, struggling for economic survival, the relatively cheaper sports-car class was almost ignored. The only event of significance was the Belgian Sports Car G. P. held in Brussels on a circuit in the Bois de la Cambre. Chiron held the lead with a T150C Talbot until its engine broke, which left the race to the Delahaye of Chaboud, followed home by the Talbots of Pierre Levegh and Raymond Sommer.

The 1946 season had been tentative and sketchy while the motor-racing world struggled to return to normality. It was a different story in 1947. Several of the national Grands Prix returned to the calendar, some on the original circuits. There was a substantial programme of lesser races, though the major sports-car events, apart from the Mille Miglia, had not yet been revived.

Eugene Chaboud took a chicane in the 1946 Marseille Grand Prix with his stripped Type 135 Delahaye.

Ettore's last design was the engine of the abortive Type 73C Bugatti.

Maurice Trintignant drove an Ecurie Gersac Delage in the 1947 Swiss Grand Prix.

Although Talbot, Delahaye and to a lesser degree Delage were carrying the French blue, the post-war socialist government felt there was a need for a new modern contender to restore former glories in Grand Prix racing. During 1946 a government grant was given to the Centre d'Etudes Techniques de l'Automobile et du Cycle (CTA) to produce a state-of-the-art Grand Prix car. Recalling his triumph 20 years before with the G. P. Delage, the CTA turned to Albert Lory, who started work on a design which was intended to be racing by the end of the 1947 season.

Other schemes were being hatched. A new car, the Guérin-de Coucy, designed by Enguerrand de Coucy and built by a subsidiary of the Air-Industrie combine, was exhibited at the Paris Salon in October 1946. It was a single-seater with a two-stage-blown eight-cylinder engine, all-independent suspension and a form of semi-automatic transmission, but nothing came of the venture.

More ambitiously Anne Rose-Itier, who had been a successful *Voiturette* Bugatti driver in the 1930s, joined forces with Walter Watney, still the managing director of Delage. Watney agreed to produce six improved versions of the 1937-38 sports D6-70 in the Delahaye works. These would be combined with 20 new 2.0-litre twin-cam four-cylinder Salmsons, based on the production S4 model, to form a 'school', organised by Rose-Itier under the title of the Union Sportive Automobile, to find new driving talent and encourage motor-racing enthusiasm in France. Suffering from shortage of funds, Mme. Rose-Itier's scheme soon fell apart. Probably only one of the Salmsons was made. Early in 1947 Watney sold the six Delages to

Louis Gérard, who formed Ecurie Gersac to race the cars.

Following some races on frozen lakes in Sweden, the proper 1947 season began at Pau where the Gersac Delages made their debut and Pierre Levegh took second place behind a 4CL Maserati. Eugene Chaboud was given the Ecurie France *monoplace* Talbot for the races at Perpignan and Marseille and beat the Maseratis while the Delages, despite their 3.0-litre engines, took several places.

Racing moved to a different plane at the revived Swiss G. P. on the Bremgarten circuit in Bern. The Type 158 Alfa Romeo team left the field breathless in its wake. The highest-placed French car was the Delage of Maurice Trintignant in seventh. It was much the same story in the Belgian G. P. at Spa. Chiron was back in the *monoplace* Talbot hoping to gain an advantage by running non-stop, benefiting from the car's low consumption and large tank, but the engine broke. The Alfas swept to another convincing win and the best-placed blue car was Trintignant's Delage in fifth place.

Chiron, with the repaired Talbot, used its consumption to advantage in the Marne G. P. at Reims. In a race without the Alfa Romeos he ran non-stop to come second, though it was close as he ran out of fuel crossing the line. The circus moved on to Albi. There was now a clear two-division season, depending on the presence of the Alfas. At Albi, where they were absent, new driver Louis Rosier made his mark in a stripped sports Talbot winning with ease by virtue of a non-stop run. The Type 155 *monoplace* V-12 Delahaye made its first post-war appearance, driven by Jean Achard, but sadly lost a rear wheel which hit a woman spectator with fatal results.

Louis Rosier was typical of the leading French drivers at that time. He was in his forties as were most of his contemporaries, while Etancelin was already in his fifties. Trintignant, at that time only 29, was a relative stripling.

The Ecurie Gersac Delage team lined up with a Delahaye and a Talbot at the formal reopening of Montlhéry in February 1947.

Grand Prix world. For Wimille, who stayed with Bugatti, it all came good in 1936 when France abandoned Grands Prix in favour of sports cars. He won the French G. P. and the Marne G. P. in a T57G Bugatti. A trip across the Atlantic secured a most profitable second place in the Vanderbilt Cup.

The 1937 season was busy for Wimille. He raced a road-equipped T59 in the French sports-car series and gained some impressive wins. He took part in the 'Million' prize contests for Bugatti at Montlhéry, taking the lesser prize and just missing the big one. Best of all he won the Le Mans 24 Hours in a T57G, gaining the first French win in this, the most classic of all races for eleven years. His talents becoming recognised, Wimille was lured away by Alfa Romeo in 1938. Political sanctions prevented more Alfa drives in 1939, so Wimille returned to Molsheim and won at Le Mans again with a T57C.

Jean-Pierre Wimille was in L'Armée de l'Air at the start of World War 2 and after the fall of France joined the Resistance. When the first post-war race meeting was held in the Bois de Boulogne in September 1945, he won the main race of the day in a T59/50 Bugatti.

Alfa Romeo recruited Wimille for the 1946, 1947 and 1948 seasons. He was the number one driver in the team of Type 158s and acknowledged as the best driver in the world at that time. Had there been a World Drivers' Championship during those years he would have been the undisputed champion.

When free of his Alfa commitments, Wimille drove a Gordini in F2 races and also in minor F1 events and scored some notable wins. He took a Gordini to South America at the close of 1948 for the winter race series. He was killed in practice for a race at Buenos Aires in January 1949. His death was a huge blow to French racing, leaving a gap which took a long time to fill.

Jean-Pierre Wimille (left) was seen with Pierre Veyron after his 1939 Le Mans win.

JEAN-PIERRE WIMILLE

Jean-Pierre Wimille was born in Paris in 1908, the son of a motoring and aviation journalist. He began racing in the deep end as his first outing was the 1930 French G. P. in which he drove a T37A Bugatti. Between 1931 and 1934 he raced various Bugattis and an Alfa Romeo, but apart from a handful of wins and places in minor races Wimille had little to show. He was signed up by Bugatti in 1934, but it was a bad time and the Molsheim company's fortunes were declining rapidly in the

Chiron, now 48, at last had his reward with a win at Comminges where he led a Talbot 1-2-3; he was followed by Yves Giraud-Cabantous in the 1939 offset car and Chaboud in a stripped sports T150C. In the Italian G. P. on a street circuit in Milan the Alfas dominated once again and Henri Louveau was the best blue finisher, coming sixth in a Delage.

At the end of September the French G. P. was revived on a circuit using part of the ring road around Lyon. Surprisingly the Alfa Romeo team did not attend, leaving a much more open race over 70 laps, a distance of 317 miles (510 km). It was expected to be a landmark in French motor racing as the CTA-Arsenal appeared for its debut. 'Arsenal' had been added to its title as it had been built in the national Arsenal munitions factory at Châtillon, outside Paris.

The all-new light-blue racer had a two-stage-blown V-8 engine and all-independent suspension, using torsion bars, clothed in sleek, rather high bodywork. Driven by Raymond Sommer, it was slow in practice and clearly handling badly. When the flag fell the CTA stood still; a drive shaft had snapped. It never raced again; it was the SEFAC story redux.

Chiron took the *monoplace* Talbot into the lead after five laps and stayed there until the flag. He seemed to be in complete command of the race, but unknown to his pursuers a head gasket had blown and he was desperately nursing the car. Giving a cheerful wave and smile to his pit on each passage, his apparent confidence outwitted the opposition. It was a good Talbot day as Chaboud and Rosier came third and fourth. The Talbot triumph went a long way to assuage the disappointment of the CTA.

Montlhéry had been reopened in the spring of 1947 but its first race, the Coupe de Salon, was held later, on 16 November, to coincide with the Paris motor show. The race had some importance as its outcome could decide the French drivers' championship. Chiron dropped out while leading, which left Giraud-Cabantous to take the flag in his offset 1939 Talbot. Several laps behind, Chaboud came second, but the result made him champion.

An excellent season for Talbot had shown that Chiron's *monoplace* was probably the best in the field behind the unbeatable Alfa Romeos. Spurred by Chiron's successes, during the winter of 1947 Antony Lago and his chief engineer Carlo Marchetti began work on an improved *monoplace*. Talbot announced that 20 of the new cars would be built for a works team and for sale to customers in 1948.

At the start of the Grand Prix d'Alsace in August 1947 number 18 was Rosier's Talbot, number 14 Pozzi's Talbot and number 16 the Talbot of Giraud-Cabantous.

Raymond Sommer attempted practice for the 1947 French Grand Prix in the tragically farcical CTA-Arsenal.

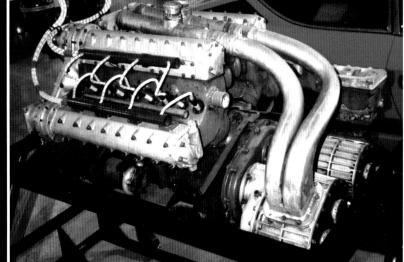

The V-8 engine of the CTA-Arsenal was the work of designer Lory.

The 1.5-litre Guerin-de-Coucy never raced.

Chiron swept to victory in the 1947 French Grand Prix at Lyon with his Lago-Talbot.

CHAPTER 13

The Talbot Years

A 1949/1950 Talbot Type 26C.

AHE new Grand Prix Talbot for 1948 had much in common with the 1939 *monoplace*. The chassis still had transverse-leaf front suspension and a live rear axle, the transmission being offset to give the driver a lower seating position. The drive shaft passed to the driver's right, the padded tunnel forming an armrest. As before there was a preselector gearbox.

The biggest change came with the engine. It had an alloy head and cylinder block with two camshafts set high in the block, operating the valves through pushrods and rockers. It was a system which had been used by British Rileys and ERAs with great success. With an engine developing about 240 bhp the new cars became the Type 26C and were known as Talbot-Lagos.

The Talbot 26C was not the only new French Grand Prix car to be announced for the 1948 season. The Dommartin engineering company declared its intention of building a car. At the beginning of 1948 the first was unveiled. It was an unblown 'V-8' with a capacity of 3.6 litres. It had sleek offset bodywork, but the penny soon dropped when it was scrutinised. It was the old SEFAC, revived with an enlarged engine and the superchargers removed, concealed by a new body. It never raced and disappeared into obscurity, together with the racing ambitions of Dommartin.

The 1948 Grand Prix season began at Pau where Giraud-Cabantous came second behind a Maserati in one of the 1939 offset Talbots. The first Type 26C went to Louis Rosier who gave it its debut at the revived Monaco G. P. Although Alfa Romeo were racing in 1948, they gave Monaco a miss. The new car did not shine and stopped, hot and steaming, after 16 laps. Still in the faithful *monoplace*, Chiron redeemed Talbot honour by taking second place on his home ground behind a Maserati and keeping on the same lap as the winner by virtue of a non-stop run.

In the Paris G. P. at Montlhéry, two weeks later, Giraud-Cabantous showed that he and the old offset car were still competitive by leading all the way, followed by Chiron whose *monoplace* had brake problems. Once again the new 26C retired amid smoke and steam. The circus moved on to San Remo in Italy where a new Maserati, the 4CLT/48,

1949 Type 26C Lago-Talbot

Benefiting from its economic fuel consumption, the 4.5-litre Type 26C Lago-Talbot was a front-runner in the late 1940s.
The greatest victory was Louis Rosier's defeat of the Ferrari team in the 1949 Belgian Grand Prix.

Anthony Lago (in raincoat), the driving force behind Talbot, discussed testing with Yves Giraud-Cabantous at Montlhéry in 1950.

Top right: The new Talbot Type 26C awaited a test at Montlhéry in 1950.

The front suspension of the Talbot Type 26C expressed its robustness.

appeared and ran away with the race. Talbot's 26C finished a race at last, in fifth place behind a new Italian entrant, a 2.0-litre Formula 2 Ferrari driven by Sommer.

The Alfa Romeos arrived at Bern for the European G. P. and as expected walked away with the race. Sadly Achille Varzi, who had worked so hard for Bugatti fifteen years before, was killed in practice when his Alfa Romeo overturned. A second 26C was driven by the Italian, Gianfranco Comotti, who had won the 1937 Tourist Trophy for Talbot. Both he and Rosier retired with broken oil pipes but Chiron took the *monoplace* into sixth, two laps behind the winner.

Two more 26Cs were finished for the French G. P. at Reims where they were driven by 'Phi-Phi' Etancelin and 'Raph', a pseudonym which took less space in the race programme than his full name, the Marquis Raphaël Béthenod de las Casas. Again the Alfas ran away from the field but Comotti, 'Raph' and Rosier took fourth, fifth and sixth places. The 26C was starting to show the adequate pace and steady reliability which would be its hallmark in coming seasons.

'Raph' and Rosier were second and fourth behind a Maserati at Comminges, separated by Chiron's *monoplace*. At Albi, a race run in two heats with aggregated results to get the overall order, 'Raph' crashed badly and fractured his skull, later making a full recovery. When the places were

added up Etancelin was second and Rosier was third behind the inevitable Maserati.

In a wet Italian G. P. held on Turin's park circuit the new Formula 1 Ferrari made its debut, taking part in a fierce battle amongst the Alfa Romeos, Maseratis and Ferraris. The pace was too hot for the 26C Talbots with Rosier, Comotti and Etancelin finishing in sixth, seventh and eighth places.

After a gap of 21 years the British G. P. was revived in October on a converted airfield at Silverstone where Rosier kept the Talbot flag flying by finishing fourth. Back in France a week later, Rosier took the 26C to its first win in the G. P. du Salon at Montlhéry while another new 26C, driven by Pierre Levegh, was second in front of Giraud-Cabantous's old offset car. This result secured the 1948 French championship for Yves Giraud-Cabantous.

A further sign of post-war recovery was the re-opening of Monza, but the 1948 Monza G. P. was another Alfa Romeo benefit. Eugene Chaboud, who had replaced his old 135 Delahaye with a new 26C, could only come sixth. Chiron too had a new 26C. After retiring at Monza he ended the season with a third place in the last race, the Pena Rhin G. P. at Barcelona. It had been a reasonably good season for the new Talbot, but changing circumstances would make it a front-runner in 1949.

French racing received a severe blow when Jean-Pierre Wimille was killed. His Gordini overturned during practice for a race in Argentina in January of 1949. At that time Wimille was considered to be the top driver in Grand Prix racing. He led the Alfa Romeo team in 1947 and 1948. Had there been a World Championship for those years he would have taken the crown. Coupled with Varzi's fatal accident, the death of team member Trossi from cancer and problems getting a new model into production, Wimille's loss prompted Alfa Romeo to announce it was withdrawing from racing in 1949.

This left the prospect of a much more open 1949 season in which the Talbots had a real chance. After races at Pau and San Remo, circuits too tight for the Talbots to shine, six 26Cs ran in the G. P.

de Paris over 50 laps of Montlhéry. It was a 1-2-3 success. Etancelin, with his unique wheel-sawing driving style, wearing a peaked cap turned back-to-front, won from Giraud-Cabantous and Belgian band leader Johnny Claes, whose car was painted in his national colour of yellow.

The British G. P. was held at Silverstone again on a course marked out with countless oil drums and straw bales. Rosier, with the advantage of a non-stop run, finished third while Etancelin was fifth. After Guy Mairesse gained a Talbot win in the minor race at Chimay in Belgium, the teams arrived in force at Spa for the Belgian G. P. The Ferrari team were the favourites while much was expected of Argentinean newcomer Juan-Manuel Fangio, who had scored several victories in a Maserati in early-season races.

Fangio soon dropped out and the Ferraris led, but their stop for tyres let Etancelin into the lead. The Ferraris soon led again, while Etancelin stopped with a broken gearbox, but a second Ferrari stop for fuel saw Louis Rosier take the

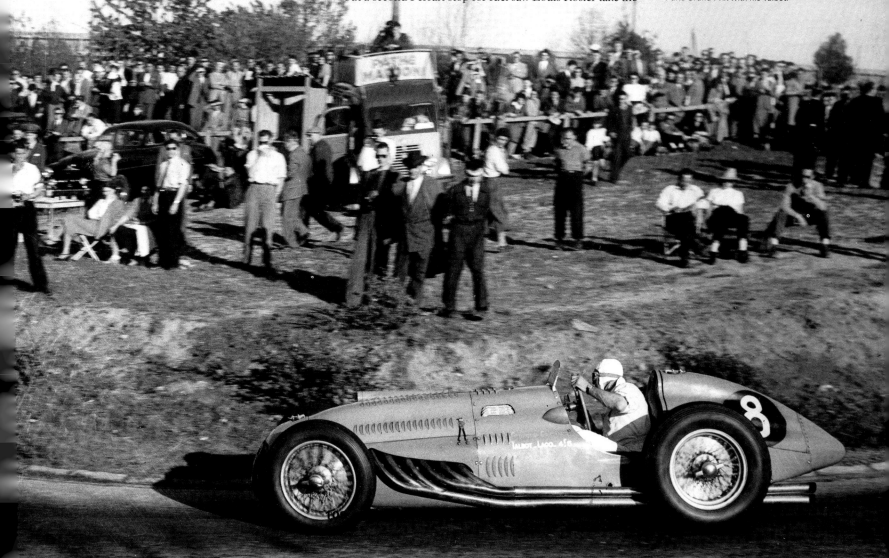

Georges Grignard pressed on to win the 1950 Paris Grand Prix with his Talbot.

LOUIS ROSIER

Louis Rosier was born in the Auvergne in 1905. He began his racing career on a Harley-Davidson motorcycle in 1927. Rosier opened a garage in Clermont-Ferrand which grew until it became one of the biggest Renault agencies in France. His first major race, following a few hill climbs, was the 1938 Le Mans 24 Hours when he drove a Talbot coupé.

After World War 2—during which he was in the Resistance and his wife and daughter were taken hostage by the Germans—Rosier began racing seriously. During 1946 he raced a stripped sports 150 Talbot gaining some minor places, his first win coming at Albi in 1947. Rosier's drives impressed Tony Lago, making him the first customer to receive the new 26C Talbot in 1948. After some disappointing retirements he scored the first win for the 26C at Montlhéry just before the end of the season.

Rosier hit top form in 1949. He took third place in the British G. P., then beat the supercharged Maseratis and Ferraris to pull off a splendid win in the Belgian G. P. at Spa. He finished the season as French champion. In 1950, the first year of the F1 World Championship, the Talbots were outclassed, though by steady driving Rosier picked up some podium places. His major win was at Le Mans. It was an individual triumph. In a sports version of the 26C he drove through the 24 hours almost single-handed, letting his son take the wheel for a mere 20 minutes.

Rosier carried on with the 26C in 1951 but gained no Grand Prix places. With the change of G. P. championship rules in 1952 Rosier moved over to Ferrari. He raced a Ferrari 500 in 1952 and 1953, then in 1954 bought a new 250F Maserati which he raced for three seasons. This produced little success and there was only one points finish in 1956. Rosier also ran a 4.5-litre 375 F1 Ferrari in the handful of races run for the earlier formula and won at Albi in 1952 and 1953.

In sports-car races Rosier stayed faithful to the sports 26C Talbot. In 1953 he retired at Le Mans but gained a most creditable fifth place in the 2,000-mile (3,000-km) Carrera Panamericana. He was signed by Scuderia Ferrari for Le Mans in 1954, but the car failed and he had no success with his 375 Ferrari converted to a sports car. In 1956 Rosier was back with Talbot, racing a Maserati-engined version at Le Mans but without success. It was a different story in the 1,000 km at Montlhéry. On a wet day Rosier and Jean Behra were the winners in a sports 300S Maserati.

Montlhéry was Rosier's last win. Driving a 3.0-litre Monza sports Ferrari he went off the road and overturned during the

Louis Rosier celebrated his win in the 1949 Belgian Grand Prix.

Coupe de Salon at Montlhéry at the end of the 1956 season. He died of his injuries three weeks later. At an age when most drivers are thinking of hanging up their helmets, the genial Rosier had begun racing seriously and scored some remarkable wins. He was French Champion for four successive years.

lead. He rumbled on steadily too far ahead to be caught. Rosier won the 315-mile (506-km) race by almost a minute from the Ferraris, amid intense jubilation from the visiting French. It was significant that his race average was 96.95 mph (155.99 km/h), while the victorious Alfa Romeo two years earlier had averaged 95.28 mph (153.30 km/h), so the Talbot wasn't a mere tortoise amongst the supercharged hares.

The Swiss G. P. on the rapid Bremgarten circuit suited the Ferraris and was only 180 miles (290 km) so the Talbots' fuel economy was less advantageous, but Sommer and Etancelin placed third and fourth. There were two

French G. P.s in 1949. One was held for sports cars at Comminges and the other, called the G. P. de France, was run at Reims.

Once again at Reims Ferraris and Maseratis battled for the lead while the Talbots waited. As the pace told and the blown cars dropped out or made fuel stops, Chiron's Talbot moved up the field and took the lead with 20 laps to go. He was repassed by Whitehead's Ferrari, but the latter's gearbox jammed in gear with eight laps to go so Chiron surged to the front and took the flag. The race had started at 5:00 p.m. and ended in the early dusk with Chiron mobbed by the crowd. It was his last major win only two weeks short of his 50th birthday. Fittingly he was in a blue car.

The sports-car French G. P. was held in early August on an intensely hot day. It saw a now-rare Delahaye win when Charles Pozzi took the flag in his obsolete Type 135. Sports-car racing was reviving, the Le Mans 24-Hour race being scheduled in June. Chaboud's Delahaye led there for four hours but then caught fire, which left a Ferrari dominating the race. It was chased by one of the former Gersac Delages, driven by Henri Louveau and Juan Jover. They closed the gap rapidly in the final hours as the Ferrari had clutch slip, but the Italian car just held on to keep the Delage in second.

It was the same story in the Spa 24 Hours two weeks later. The Ferrari led, chased again by the Delage, which Louveau was sharing with Edmond Mouche. About 20

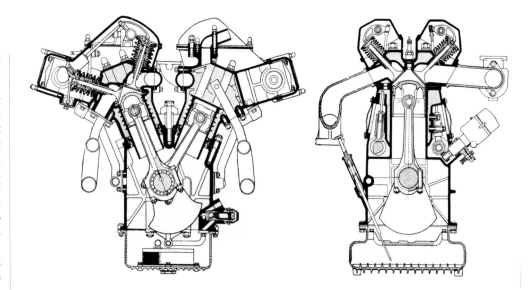

Among Talbot engines, on the left the 1939 V-16 was not built and on the right the six-cylinder Type 26C.

minutes before the end the Delage began to spew oil. The Ferrari spun on it and went off the road. The battered Ferrari was pushed back on to the track and staggered to the finish, less than a lap ahead of the oily and ailing Delage.

A 12-plug cylinder head developed at Suresnes gave the Talbot-Lago an increase in power. Fitted to Etancelin's Talbot, it took him to second place in 1949's European G. P. at Monza behind a new and quicker Ferrari. Etancelin went on to Brno where he came second behind a Ferrari in the Czech G. P. The season finished at Montlhéry where

A similar car to this Talbot Type 26C in sports-racing form won the Le Mans 24 Hours in 1950.

The start of the 1950 French Grand Prix at Reims found the Talbots of Etancelin and Giraud-Cabantous in the second row behind the all-conquering Type 158 Alfa Romeos.

Sommer led a Talbot 1-2-3-4 in the G. P. du Salon.

It had been a marvellous season for the French-blue Talbot-Lagos, which looked like proper racing cars. Driven by greying, middle-aged men, they'd put France right back on the Grand Prix map. However the game was about to change once more. Grand Prix racing was to enter a new era.

Introduced in 1950, the World Championship for Drivers changed the form of Grand Prix racing forever. The year also saw the return of Alfa Romeo. The Talbots had influenced the thinking of Enzo Ferrari, who abandoned superchargers and introduced a 4.5-litre unsupercharged V-12 which ended Alfa Romeo's dominance.

The Talbots were back to the same role they had in earlier years, as a supporting cast of also-rans. They had one passing moment of glory. In the Belgian G. P. at Spa, the Alfa Romeo team underestimated the speed of Sommer's Talbot-Lago, which took the lead when the Alfas stopped for fuel. Sommer stayed in front until the Talbot's engine broke. Sommer was then the fastest of the French drivers so it was a huge blow when he was killed in a minor race later in the season.

Rosier gained two wins at Albi and in the non-championship Dutch G. P. at Zandvoort. He also managed a second place at Pescara when the Alfas wilted slightly. The 26C Talbot was no slouch, as Rosier was timed at 166 mph (267 km/h) over a kilometre at Pescara. At the end of the year three Talbots went to Argentina for a 500-mile race at Rafaela. One was driven by Juan Fangio, who came home the winner, followed by Rosier.

A 26C Talbot had been converted into a sports car with narrow two-seat cycle-winged coachwork. Rosier took this to Le Mans for the 1950 24-Hour race. His son Jean-Louis was the nominal co-driver but apart from a mere 20 minutes, Rosier drove the entire race himself. He took the lead at midnight as the faster Ferraris fell by the wayside. In the early hours of Sunday morning, Rosier spent half an hour in the pits while a broken rocker arm was changed.

This let the lead pass to the veteran 1939 offset Talbot, now a sports car, driven by Pierre Meyrat and Guy Mairesse. By mid-morning, Rosier was in front again with a lap lead. He stayed there to the finish while the other Talbot was second. The win was a great delight for France and a considerable recompense for the fading hopes of Talbot in Grands Prix.

In 1951 there was little room for Talbot amidst a titanic battle between Alfa Romeo and Ferrari in the World Championship rounds. Rosier gained wins at Bordeaux and Zandvoort but had little to show in the major races. At Le Mans Rosier co-drove with Fangio, but their pseudo-sports Talbot fell by the wayside. At the end of 1951 the 1.5-litre supercharged vs. 4.5-litre unsupercharged Grand Prix formula was effectively abandoned. The FIA agreed that the World Championship would be contested by 2.0-litre unsupercharged cars which had been racing as the supporting Formula 2. It was the end for the magnificent 26C Talbots which now could race only in minor events.

Five sports 26Cs had been built with all-enveloping bodies which gave them an up-to-date appearance, even if the underlying design with its live rear axle was obsolete. In 1952 Mercedes-Benz returned to racing with a team of 300SL coupés. The German team ran at Le Mans, but after the faster Jaguars and a Gordini dropped out, Pierre Levegh took the lead with a 26C. Driving single-handed, as the race progressed he pulled out a commanding lead over the team of 300SLs.

It was a bitter blow for Levegh and *la belle France* when, with an hour of the race to run, the over-revved engine broke a con rod, leaving the German 300SLs to take first and second places. Levegh, whose real name was Pierre Bouillin, was the nephew of 'Levegh' who had raced Mors successfully in the early years of the century. There was a tragic sequel. Alfred Neubauer, the Mercedes-Benz team manager, asked Levegh to drive a 300SLR Mercedes at Le Mans in 1955. His car crashed into the crowd killing 81 spectators; Levegh also died in the accident.

The sports 26Cs gained some successes. One was a win in the 1952 Casablanca 12-Hours by Charles Pozzi and Lucien Vincent. In 1953 Rosier came second in the Reims 12-Hours—but it was the end of the Talbot story. Anthony Lago died in 1960 aged 68. He had said with justifiable pride, 'No one was ever killed in my cars.' Louis Rosier, who had contributed so much to the Talbot successes, carried on racing with Ferrari and Maserati. He died of his injuries when he crashed in the Coupe du Salon at Montlhéry in October 1956, two weeks short of his 51st birthday.

Pierre Levegh in his sports Type 150C Talbot led a 300SL Mercedes at Le Mans in 1952. In front with an hour to go, the Talbot's engine broke, letting the Mercedes-Benz team take a 1-2 victory.

CHAPTER 14

The Sorcerer's Magic

Like Bugatti and Lago, Amédée Gordini was an Italian in France.

ASTRONG Italian influence has prevailed in French motor racing. Like Ettore Bugatti and Anthony Lago, Amédée Gordini was Italian by birth. As Amedeo he was born at Bazzano, between Modena and Bologna, in 1899. He was apprenticed as a youth in a local Fiat agency under Edoardo Weber, later to be famous as a carburettor manufacturer, then moved to Isotta-Fraschini where his foreman was Alfieri Maserati. He served in the Italian army in World War 1 and was a keen boxer.

After the war, convinced that Paris was the centre of the sporting world—and still with boxing ambitions—Gordini moved there and found work as a mechanic. In 1925 he started his own motor business in workshops opposite the Talbot factory in the Avenue de la République. He obtained a Fiat agency and in 1929 became a French citizen.

Gordini began competing with a 514 Fiat tourer and in 1935 moved on to a sports 508S Fiat Balilla. With this he gained some notable wins, including the 1935 24-hour Bol d'Or, where drivers had to go the whole distance single-handed. By the end of the 1936 season he was almost unbeatable in the 1,100 cc class.

In 1935 the manufacture of Fiats under licence had begun in France at Nanterre, west of Paris by Simca (Societé Industrielle et Méchanique et Carrossiere Automobile). In 1936 Gordini signed a contract with Simca which gave him considerable support. During the autumn of 1936 he received two Simca-Fiat 500 Topolinos which he fitted with light-weight sports bodywork and prepared for racing and record-breaking. One of the Topolinos won the 750 cc class at Le Mans in 1937 while Gordini continued his run of successes with the Balilla. At the end of the season the Topolino took 750 cc class records at Montlhéry up to 48 hours and 4,000 miles.

Simca was now building its version of the 508C 1100 Fiat, two chassis of which were sent to Gordini. These were tuned, slightly modified and fitted with light-weight all-enveloping bodies. Both failed at Le Mans but the Topolinos won the 750 cc class again. One of the 508Cs driven by Gordini redeemed itself with a class win in the Spa 24 Hours while the second car won its class in the Tourist Trophy.

A third 508C was built up for the 1939 season with even sleeker bodywork. Driven by Gordini himself and José Scaron, this took the 1,100 cc class at Le Mans and—better still—won the Coupe Biennale for success two years in a row, which was then considered to offer almost the prestige of an outright win.

The war years were bleak. Like so many Frenchmen, Gordini kept his head down while waiting and hoping for better things. He took over a garage and workshop in the Boulevard Victor and moved some of his cars and machine tools there. It was a fortunate move as the workshops in the Rue de la République were destroyed in an air raid in 1943. Gordini entered his 1939 car for the Coupe Robert Benoist, the first race on the programme at the meeting held in the Bois de Boulogne in September 1945. He won the 36-lap race easily, so had the distinction of winning the first European race to be held after World War 2.

During the war years Gordini had discussed with Dante Giacosa, the Fiat designer, the creation of a *monoplace* racer based on Simca-Fiat 1100 parts. This was built during the winter of 1945-46. It had a 1.1-litre engine, a tubular chassis frame, Simca coil-spring front suspension and a live rear axle. Covered with a neat *monoplace* body, it became known as the T11. Although no proper *Voiturette* formula had been established it was generally agreed that the class would be for supercharged cars up to 1,100 cc or 2.0 litres unsupercharged.

The first race was at Nice on Easter Sunday of 1946. Gordini drove the T11 while Scaron had the 1939 car. Though Gordini went off the road Scaron won, so the team had begun well. Gordini scored the first win for the T11 at Marseilles two weeks later and followed it with another win at St. Etienne. He retired at St Cloud, where Scaron won again, but went on to win at Dijon and Nantes.

The team went to the Belgian Sports Car G. P. in Brussels. Running in the 1,100 cc race, Gordini went off the road in the 1939 car but recovered to take second place, while Scaron was third in the 1938 sports car. A second T11 was finished in August 1946. The two single-seaters went to the 1,100 cc curtain-raiser for the Turin G. P. in September. There they met the new Fiat-based Cisitalia. Both Gordinis retired, but Scaron came eighth with the 1939 car.

Encouraged by his successes and with the full support of Simca, Gordini built three more T11s for the 1947 season. With the results he had achieved Gordini was now widely known as 'Le Sorcier'—'The Sorcerer'—and the small company was now accepted as a serious contender in the *Voiturette* class, which had become a recognised part of the European scene.

Gordini signed Jean-Pierre Wimille, then the leading French driver, and Maurice Trintignant as his drivers for 1947. They were later joined by the Siamese Prince Bira who had been a leading *Voiturette* driver with ERA in the late 1930s. Gordini had ambitions to enter Formula 1. To this end a 1.5-litre supercharged V-8 engine was designed by Gioachino Colombo, who had just finished designing the first V-12 Ferrari. There was also an alternative 4.5-litre

Prince Bira dominated the 1947 Manx Cup with his Type 11 Gordini.

unit designed and built by the Maserati brothers, but his Simca paymasters told Gordini to forget such ambitions and carry on with the Simca-based cars.

Two more cars were built, using a 1,220 cc engine, which became the T15. Wimille took the T15 to Pau, the first Gordini entry in a Formula 1 race, but it retired with clutch bothers while amongst the leaders. He was also amidst the leaders at Perpignan until the car overheated. As the lead driver for Alfa Romeo, Wimille moved on to higher things when the full Grand Prix season began. Still available to race in the *Voiturette* class, he won for Gordini at Nimes.

Jean Behra (left) conversed with team-mate Juan Manuel Fangio at Sebring in 1955.

JEAN BEHRA

Jean Behra was born in Nice in 1921. As a teenager he began racing motorcycles and after World War 2 rapidly rose to the top. Riding a Moto Guzzi he won four national titles. His first car race was at Montlhéry where he took sixth place in the 1949 G. P. du Salon with a 26C Talbot. Impressive runs in the 1950 Monte Carlo Rally and in the Bol d'Or attracted the attention of Amédée Gordini, who gave him a works drive at Le Mans. In 1951 there were occasional drives for Gordini. In mid-season Behra showed he meant business with third places in the F2 races at Sables d'Olonne and Cadours.

Jean Behra became the Gordini team leader in 1952, fighting magnificently against the more powerful Ferrari team in the 2.0-litre races that now comprised the World Championship. He was acclaimed as the hero of France when he defeated the Ferrari team on the ultra-fast circuit at Reims. The pace was getting too hot for the under-financed Gordini team and Behra had little to show in 1953. It was worse still in 1954 when a fresh generation of cars appeared for the new 2.5-litre Formula 1. A Gordini with a bored-out engine was wholly uncompetitive. Behra's only wins came in the non-championship races at Pau, Cadours and Montlhéry.

Realising that Gordini was a busted flush, Behra moved to Maserati in 1955. With a 250F there were podium places, but his season ended with an unpleasant accident with a 300S sports Maserati in the Tourist Trophy on the dangerous Dundrod circuit when he lost an ear in a crash. Undaunted, he was back in a 250F for the 1956 season, picking up a string of podium places and taking fourth spot in the World Championship. There was a win in the 1,000 km at Montlhéry, sharing the car with Louis Rosier.

There were not so many places in 1957, at the end of which Behra left Maserati and joined the enigmatic and erratic British BRM team. He had already driven a BRM during 1956, in non-championship races at Caen and Silverstone, and won both. With the move to BRM not fruitful, for 1959 Behra accepted an offer from Enzo Ferrari. It was not a happy relationship. After a punch-up with team manager Tavoni at the French G. P. Behra left the Prancing Horse.

Jean Behra had been driving his own Porsche in F2 races. In August of 1959 he ran this in the German G. P. at the Avus. Behra went over the top of the notorious north banking and was killed instantly. He was a tough, talented driver and it was surprising that he never won a World Championship round. In France, though, his Gordini-mounted day of glory at Reims was never forgotten.

cars. Apart from some wins in minor sports-car races there was little to show. There was a finish at Le Mans, where a T20-engined T15 won the 3.0-litre class and was sixth overall.

The Grand Prix formula changed in 1954, becoming 2.5 litres unsupercharged and only 750 cc blown. Initially all Gordini could do was bore out the T20 engine, which then became the T23. Yet despite the poverty at Boulevard Victor, a straight-eight engine and new chassis with all-independent suspension were designed for the new formula.

In the 1954 World Championship rounds, facing Ferrari, Maserati and Mercedes-Benz, Gordini could do nothing. Behra won minor races at Pau and Cadours and there was a class success at Le Mans; that was all. The 1955 season was curtailed after the Le Mans accident. The new

eight-cylinder T32 appeared in July but didn't race until the Italian G. P. at Monza in September. It was a sleek-looking car with, for the first time in a Gordini, independent rear suspension.

While waiting for the new car, the team struggled on with its old T16s. Behra, realising Gordini was a lost cause, joined Maserati at the end of 1954; he was killed in 1959 racing his Porsche on the Avus track in Berlin. Manzon carried on, supported at Gordini by a string of lesser drivers. Well off the pace, the new T32 lasted for eight laps at Monza.

There was no real improvement in 1956. Struggling to keep racing and balance his books, Gordini built a second T32. Unreliable, when the T32 lasted it was little quicker than the old T16s. To general surprise Manzon won the non-championship Naples G. P. with a T16 after the Ferraris and Maseratis had broken down.

The Gordini team appeared at the start of the 1957 season, but after the minor Naples G. P. in April it was all over. Amédée Gordini realised the battle was lost and withdrew from racing. It had been a brave struggle against the odds. Though he never had sufficient funds, he carried the French blue valiantly. With better support it would surely have been a different story. Gordini joined Renault as a consultant, advising on improved road cars and the successful Alpine rally cars. He died in 1979.

A last faint flash of French blue flared during the 1950s. Roland Bugatti, Ettore's surviving son, had kept the company going with the help of Pierre Marco. In 1956 a Grand Prix Bugatti appeared again. Designed by Gioachino Colombo, the T251 had an in-line eight-cylinder engine mounted transversely behind its driver and solid axles at front and rear. The bulky-looking T251 made one racing appearance at Reims for the 1956 French G. P., driven by Trintignant. It was slow, handled uncertainly and lasted only a few laps. The project was abandoned and it never raced again. French blue was about to enter a long, bleak decade.

Top right: The advanced Sascha Gordine never raced. Backer Sascha Gordine stands in the middle of the group.

Trintignant drove the last Grand Prix Bugatti, the Type 251, at Reims in 1956. The two Type 251 Bugattis constructed now reside in the Mulhouse Museum.

Robert Manzon's T32 Gordini led the D50 Lancia-Ferrari of Peter Collins in the 1956 British Grand Prix.

CHAPTER 15

Aerospace Racers

THROUGHOUT the late 1950s and early 1960s Europe's racing circuits were dominated by Italian red and British green cars. French blue vanished from Grand Prix tracks. In sports-car racing the only activity was in small-capacity classes. From the humble machines racing in these categories came the French-blue renaissance.

A 1951 Le Mans DB-Panhard.

Charles Deutsch and René Bonnet had a mutual interest in motor racing; Deutsch a civil engineer with skills in aerodynamics and Bonnet a gifted mechanical engineer. In the 1930s they began producing a handful of sports-racing cars based on 11CV Citroën *Traction Avant* components. These were raced in 1938 and 1939 with limited success, but were notable for advanced aerodynamics.

Panhard, which had slipped from its eminence as a maker of large luxury cars in the 1920s, after World War 2 went to the other extreme. It started making a twin-cylinder 610 cc front-drive saloon, the Dyna, which made much use of aluminium in its structure. Deutsch and Bonnet formed DB to use the Panhard components to make neat 750 cc sports-racers.

From 1949 onwards the DB dominated the 750 cc class. There were class wins at Le Mans, Sebring and in the Mille Miglia, an Index of Performance victory at Le Mans and an outright win in the 1954 Tourist Trophy when it was run as a handicap race on the Dundrod circuit in Northern Ireland. From 1957 DB carried the French blue almost alone on the international circuits.

In the 1930s CAPRA, an aircraft engineering sub-contractor, was formed by Marcel Chassagny. It became Méchanique Aviation Traction (Matra) which, after World

War 2, as well as fulfilling aircraft subcontracts began making guided missiles. Chassagny helped DB with an injection of capital. In 1961 Deutsch and Bonnet split. Deutsch continued as a consultant and Bonnet continued competition-car production. When this faltered, Chassagny bought out Bonnet.

A car division of Engins Matra—now a major industrial group—was established to carry on production of the Djet, a sports coupé designed by Bonnet with a Gordini-developed Renault engine. The Djet enjoys a place in history as one of the very first road cars to have a mid-mounted engine. To give Matra more sporting appeal and to get the benefits of rapid advances in the sport's technology, Matra decided to go motor racing.

Matra chose as its point of entry a successor to Formula Junior, which had been established in 1958 as a basic formula to encourage new drivers. Using production-based 1,000 cc and 1,100 cc engines, by the early 1960s it had burgeoned into a major class, second only to Formula 1. In 1963, with slight changes to the rules, it became Formula 3. Matra decided to enter Formula 3.

The class was dominated by the British-built Ford Cosworth engine and so abandoning national pride, the MS 1 Matra was built using the Ford engine. Its quality of construction, with a riveted aluminium monocoque chassis, brought new standards to Formula 3. To huge French delight a Matra won the Formula 3 race supporting the 1965 French G. P. at Reims. Driven by Jean-Pierre Beltoise, a motorcycle-racing champion, it beat the previously all-conquering British cars. Beltoise went on to become the 1965 French Formula 3 champion.

A subsidiary Formula 2, using full-race 1,000 cc engines, was established in 1964. One of its leading players was the Scottish driver, Jackie Stewart, with a BRM-engined Cooper. Entered and prepared by former racing driver Ken Tyrrell, it was virtually the Cooper works entry. The talented Stewart's career was blossoming rapidly and he was in the BRM Formula 1 team.

In 1965 the Cooper-BRM had a poor season in Formula 2. Matra wanted to move up, so Ken Tyrrell was persuaded to run a team of Matra MS5s, a development of the MS1, using the BRM engine for the 1966 Formula 2 season. Matra also entered a team with Beltoise and Frenchman Jo Schlesser as drivers. The results were promising, gaining several places in a full Formula 2 season. Matra made a first appearance in a World Championship race when Beltoise ran in the Formula 2 class in the German G. P. at the Nürburgring and came home the class winner, finishing eighth overall.

This 1,191 cc Panhard-engined CD ran at Le Mans in 1964.

Seen in his Matra-Ford DFV MS 80 at Monaco in 1969, Jackie Stewart went on to become 1969 World Champion.

This Matra M630/650 competed at Watkins Glen in 1969.

Ken Tyrrell's team took Matra to the Constructors' Championship in 1969.

In 1967 Formula 2 changed to 1,600 cc unsupercharged. A new Matra, the MS7, became a leading contender using a Ford-Cosworth engine. Beltoise, Stewart and Jacky Ickx, the Belgian, who had joined the Tyrrell team, all scored wins and Ickx was the European Formula 2 champion. This prepared the ground for a move to racing's top rung.

Matra made the decision to enter Formula 1. The French national oil company Elf agreed to back the project and—in an echo of efforts just before and after the war—the French government provided six million francs. Georges Martin came from Simca to design a V-12 engine. Meanwhile, Stewart had become disenchanted with BRM and agreed to join Tyrrell for the 1968 season.

Tyrrell took over a new Matra MS10 chassis, designed by Bernard Boyer, and fitted it with a British DFV Ford-Cosworth which, when it appeared in 1967, immediately set new standards in Formula 1. After a tentative start, suffering handling problems and delays caused by an injured hand, Stewart and the Matra-Ford came good. In the Dutch G. P. at Zandvoort he gained an impressive win. A development programme was starting for the V-12, which was driven into second place by Beltoise. The Dutch victory marked the first time a French-blue car had won a World Championship round.

Stewart went on to win the German and United States G. P.s to take third place in the Drivers' Championship while Matra was third in the Constructors' Championship.

To round off Matra's success, Beltoise and Henri Pescarolo took their MS7s to first and second places in the European Formula 2 Championship. After nearly 20 years, French blue was back in the forefront of motor racing.

As a back-up to its Grand Prix ambitions Matra had also entered sports-car racing. A team of three M620 coupés with 2.0-litre V-8 BRM engines ran at Le Mans in 1966, but all retired. An improved car, the MS630, still with the BRM engine, appeared at Le Mans in 1967, but had no success. Hopes were then pinned on the V-12 engine, which made its sports-car debut in the MS630 in 1968's 1,000 km at Spa. The race started in a downpour and the car stopped after a lap with swamped ignition. It lasted for 22 hours at Le Mans, running as high as second before a tyre blew out and the electrics failed.

Matra's year was 1969. Probably wisely, it decided that the V12-engine should be reserved for the sports cars. A new, lighter Grand Prix chassis, the MS80, was built with emphasis on improving the handling. In line with several other F1 teams, a four-wheel-drive chassis was built with the aim of getting all the benefits of the power given by the Ford DFV engine. Bizarre aerodynamic wings for downforce arrived in F1 in 1968 and Matra joined the craze.

Stewart began the season by winning the first championship round in South Africa with the MS10-Ford. The MS80 came out for the Spanish G. P., which Stewart won. The Scotsman then pulled off a hat-trick of wins in the Dutch, French and British G. P.s. The French win on the demanding Charade circuit was especially satisfying as Beltoise backed up Stewart by finishing second. A second place in the German G. P. on the Nürburgring and an Italian G. P. win at Monza secured Stewart the World Championship.

The Monza race was dramatic with slip-streaming all the way. On the last lap it was a battle to the line. Stewart beat Jochen Rindt's Lotus by a mere 0.08 second while Beltoise in third was only 0.17 seconds behind! Satisfying French pride, even more so than Stewart's Championship triumph, Matra was the Constructors' Champion. To heighten the triumph of French blue, Johnny Servoz-Gavin took the European F2 Championship with an MS7. Raced by Beltoise in two Championship rounds, the four-wheel-drive MS84 seemed to give little advantage.

In recognition of the origin of some of the funding, the sports MS650 V-12 Matras were entered as Matra-Simcas in 1969. Though an MS640 designed by Robert Choulet, who had worked with Charles Deutsch, was destroyed in a practice crash at Le Mans, a revised design, the MS650, went to the 24-hour race. Three cars ran, battling with the

Ford GT40s and Porsches. The Matras lacked the ultimate pace to win but came a creditable fourth, fifth and seventh.

A month later the M650 recorded a fourth place in the Watkins Glen Six Hours in the USA. The season ended with a most encouraging home win when the MS650s came first and second in the relatively minor 1,000 km at Montlhéry. The sports cars had not achieved quite so much, but were going in the right direction.

With its 1969 Championship wins and the improving sports cars, Matra was fired up for 1970. Ken Tyrrell was told that he and Stewart must use the V-12 engine. Both had doubts about deserting the trusty DFV, so the pair departed to race a March and later Tyrrell's own creations, securing two more Championships for Stewart.

Matra's F1 car was now entered as a Matra-Simca. This tied up with a deal made with Chrysler—which had taken over Simca—to supply power trains for the planned Matra Bagheera road car. Georges Martin reworked the V-12 engine and installed it in a new monocoque designed by Bernard Boyer, becoming the MS120.

Sadly, the magic had gone. Beltoise and Pescarolo had been signed as the all-French driver team, but the best they could do was three third places. Though the V-12 made a superb and memorable sound, it was no more powerful than the DFV and less reliable. There were no rewards in F2. The MS7 was outdated and no new design appeared.

The sports-car world also showed an unfriendly face. With the major races run for the Manufacturers' Championship favouring so-called production 5.0-litre cars like Ford GT40s, the 3.0-litre Matras were at a

disadvantage. They ran in a limited season. Triple World Champion Jack Brabham, now at the end of his career, joined the team, but apart from another win at the Montlhéry 1,000 km there was little to show. At Le Mans all three cars retired almost simultaneously, after seven hours, with engine disasters.

The New Zealand driver Chris Amon left Ferrari to replace Pescarolo at Matra in 1971. Amon has been described as the greatest driver never to win a World Championship round; unfortunately this was his continuing story at Matra. There were high hopes at the beginning of the season when Amon won the non-championship Argentine G. P. Despite the appearance of an improved MS120B, the only placing thereafter was a third in the Spanish G. P.

Despite the Argentine win, the Matra team received a setback during that trip. A sports MS660 was raced in the Buenos Aires 1,000 km. It ran out of fuel during the race and was hit by the Ferrari of Ignazio Giunti while Beltoise was pushing back to the pits. Giunti succumbed to his injuries and although Beltoise was unhurt, his race licence was suspended for a while. This accident and the concentration on F1 diminished Matra's sports-car effort. One car ran at Le Mans only to fall by the wayside.

With national prestige at stake a fresh effort was demanded. In 1972 most of the effort in the Matra factory at Vélizy-Villacoublay, in the south-western Paris suburbs, went into the sports MS660. The sports-car championship rules had adopted a limit of 3.0 litres, the same as Formula 1, so competitors could use the same basic

Chris Amon drove Matra's V-12 MS 120B at the 1971 United States Grand Prix.

Matra's first Le Mans victory came in 1973, with the MS 670B winning the 24 Hours.

HENRI PESCAROLO

Henri Pescarolo has an unique record in motor-racing history, having competed in the Le Mans 24-Hour race 33 times and been a four-time winner. Pescarolo—'Pesca'—was among the first of the new generation of French drivers who appeared after the empty years of the 1950s. Born in 1942, the son of a surgeon, he began by following in his father's footsteps but abandoned his medical studies after he participated in the 1964 competition organised by *Sport Auto* with Lotus Sevens to encourage new French driving talent. Pescarolo didn't win the top prize but his talent was spotted.

In 1965 Pescarolo joined the Matra F3 team. He took the European F3 title in 1967 and was promoted to the company's F2 team the following season, becoming runner-up in the 1968 F2 Championship. He entered F1 in 1968 with the Matra team but had little success and moved to Williams in 1971. His subsequent Grand Prix years with March, BRM and Surtees yielded almost nothing.

Matra meanwhile embarked on an ambitious sports-racing programme. Pescarolo was in at the start with abortive runs at Le Mans in 1966, 1967 and 1968. A massive effort saw a Matra win in the legendary 24 Hours in 1972 when Pescarolo shared the winning car with British double World Champion Graham Hill. Matra had a full season in sports-car-championship races in 1973 and Pescarolo won five races including Le Mans again. At the end of the season he received national recognition by his appointment to the Legion d'Honneur. Results were even better in 1974. Driving the Matra 670C, Pescarolo won nine sports-car-championship rounds which included his Le Mans hat trick.

After Matra withdrew from racing Pescarolo's expertise was much in demand. Alfa Romeo signed him for 1975 and he won three sports-car-championship rounds in a Type 33. After that he began a shuttle between Porsche and assorted makes. Three Porsche wins came in 1978 and another in 1980. He took the French-built Rondeau-Ford to victory at Monza in 1982, then in 1984 notched his fourth Le Mans win, this time with Porsche. When the Swiss-German Sauber team recruited his talents he responded with a win at the Nürburgring in 1986. There were also drives for the British Jaguar and Spice teams. Pescarolo's last win came with a Porsche in the 1991 Daytona 24 Hours.

Henri Pescarolo continued to race, though less frequently, until the end of the 1990s. From 1994 he drove a Courage-Porsche, made at Le Mans by Yves Courage. His last race was at Le Mans in 1999 when he finished ninth. In 2000 he founded Pescarolo Sport, forming a team of sports-racers using Courage chassis with turbo Peugeot engines. Running in the FIA World Sports-Car Championship series, his cars scored wins in 2002 at Estoril and Magny-Cours.

Two more wins came in 2003 before Peugeot stopped the engine supply and took away important sponsorship. The Courage chassis were extensively modified and V-10 engines came from the British Judd company for 2004. The Judd engines took the Pescarolo team to wins in the Le Mans Endurance Championship in 2005 and 2006. In 2007 Pescarolo Automobiles was formed and Judd-engined sports-racing cars were offered for sale. A Pescarolo finished third at Le Mans.

It seems that the name is likely to figure in sports-car racing for the foreseeable future. As driver, builder and entrant Henri Pescarolo holds an unique and honoured place in the history of French blue.

engines. This being Matra's chance, the company decided to concentrate the sports-car effort solely on Le Mans.

The MS660 evolved with improved aerodynamics to become the MS670, and three were entered at Le Mans. The outlook was even brighter when the Ferrari team withdrew shortly before the race. Such were expectations that the tricolour to start the race was waved by President Pompidou. It all ended happily, the MS670s dominating the race despite minor problems.

Shrewdly, team manager Claude LeGuezec arranged for each car to have a French driver. The winning car was driven by Henri Pescarolo and British double World Champion Graham Hill. François Cevert and New Zealander Howden Ganley were second and the MS670 of Jean-Pierre Jabouille and Briton David Hobbs was fourth.

Rejoicing was unrestrained. French blue had triumphed in the world's premier sports-car race after a 22-year hiatus.

In F1 Matra's ambitions were waning. Amon was retained as the sole driver in 1972. Bernard Boyer reworked the MS120B into the MS120C but this offered little challenge. Boyer then produced the MS120D. With a new shape and better weight distribution, it looked promising. In the French G. P. at Charade Amon led until slowed by a puncture at half-distance, but still finished third. That was the high point of 1972. After that there was only a fourth in the British G. P.

At the end of the season the Chrysler-Simca paymasters decided that there was a better return from sports-car racing and the career of the F1 Matra was ended. Although the later years had been less good than were hoped, Stewart's Championship in 1969 had put French blue back on top of motor racing.

Matra launched an all-out attack on the World Sports-Car Championship in 1973. The MS670 became the MS670B with the British Hewland gearbox replaced by a Porsche design. After a disappointing start at Daytona, Pescarolo and Gérard Larrousse won on the Vallelunga circuit outside Rome. The pair repeated the victory in the Dijon 1,000 km, then came third at Monza and at Spa. There was a worrying setback at the Nürburgring when the engines of both MS670Bs burst, with Le Mans only two weeks ahead.

Le Mans was a fierce battle with the Ferraris and for once it was the Italian cars that wilted. In the closing stages Pescarolo and Larrousse suffered an agonising delay when the starter motor jammed, but pressed on to win. To add to French exultation they went on to win in both Austria and New York State at Watkins Glen. Their results gave Matra the Sports-Car Championship. A grateful French nation honoured Pescarolo and Larrousse with appointment to the Legion d'Honneur.

Matra returned to sports cars again in 1974. It looked easy as Ferrari had decided to concentrate on F1. This expectation was fulfilled. After failure at Monza, the MS670Cs—using the Hewland gearbox again—won at Spa, the Nürburgring and Imola. At Le Mans the hat-trick was completed. Pescarolo and Larrousse won again while Jabouille and François Migault were third. The triumphal progress continued with wins at the Österreichring, Watkins Glen, Paul Ricard, Brands Hatch and in South Africa at Kylami. It was a magnificent tour de force and Matra won the Championship for the second year.

Matra's hard-headed bosses looked at the results and concluded that enough had been done. Matra was at the top, French honour and the glory of French blue had been restored. The racing division at Matra was closed at the end of 1974 with results that fully justified the nine years of effort. But the last had not been heard of the thrilling sound of the Matra V-12.

Gérard Larrousse and Henri Pescarolo celebrate after their 1974 Le Mans win.

The Matra MS 670B that Gérard Larrousse and Henri Pescarolo drove to victory at Le Mans in 1974.

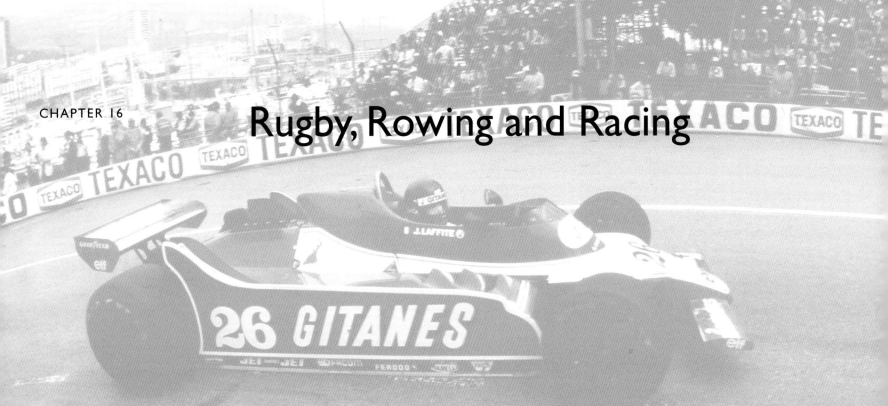

CHAPTER 16

Rugby, Rowing and Racing

GUY LIGIER was born in Vichy in 1930. When he was 13 he was apprenticed to a butcher, but he had a passion for sport. During the summer months he rowed and in the winter he played rugby. Ligier rose to eminence in both sports, becoming French coxed-pairs champion and playing for the France B rugby team.

Leaving the butchers' trade, Ligier bought a bulldozer. With this he began construction work and prospered quickly. Within a few years he had a large company for which, when the building of autoroutes began, he secured contracts and amassed a fortune.

Cars were a Ligier passion as well. He raced motorcycles in the 1950s then—encouraged by friend and business partner Jo Schlesser—moved on to Porsches in GT races. In 1966 he upgraded to F1 with a light-blue Cooper-Maserati. His best result was a sixth in the 1967 German G. P. After racing in lesser formulae Ligier decided to build a car of his own. He commissioned Michel Tétu to

design a Ford-powered sports coupé, the JS1–JS in memory of Jo Schlesser, who was killed in the 1968 French G. P.

After Ligier drove the JS1 at Le Mans in 1970 it was reworked into the Maserati-powered JS2. Fitted with a DFV Ford-Cosworth engine, at Le Mans in 1975 this almost pulled off victory as the winning Gulf-Mirage was ailing and finished only a lap ahead of the Ligier.

Guy Ligier had bigger ambitions. When Matra pulled out at the end of 1974 he persuaded Gitanes, the French government-owned tobacco company, to back him in F1. Elf also agreed to give support, so Ligier was able to obtain the use of the V-12 Matra engine. Gérard Decarouge, who had worked with Bernard Boyer at Matra, and other members of the Matra team moved to the Ligier works at Vichy and produced the JS5, which was a virtual development of the earlier Matra MS120D.

Meanwhile, the V-12 Matra engine had been supplied to the British Shadow team, which used it for two races in 1975 without success. The Ligier F1 team began racing in

The road version of the Ligier JS2 used various engines. With Maserati power it ran at Le Mans in 1972, 1973 and 1974.

1976, which was a reasonably successful season with driver Jacques Laffite taking a second place and two thirds in World Championship races.

Matra produced a new engine for 1977, the MS76, which went into a much sleeker JS7. After a tentative start to the season all came good in Sweden; Laffite came home to win after the leading Lotus ran out of fuel. It was a landmark victory, the first-ever for an all-French car in the World Championship. Hopes ran high, but for the rest of the 1977 season Laffite achieved little else except a second place in Holland.

The 1978 season began with the Ligier JS7 which was soon replaced by the JS9 with a new gearbox and better aerodynamics. The Matra engines were now reliable but lacked ultimate pace. Laffite posted two retirements and picked up two third places. At the end of the season Matra called it a day, telling Ligier there would be no more engines.

The wheel had turned full circle. Matra had begun with the DFV Ford-Cosworth engine and now Ligier went back to it. Gérard Ducarouge and Michel Beaujon designed a new chassis, the JS11, which took Ligier into the ground-

The Ligier JS2 came second at Le Mans 1975, using a Ford DFV engine.

o

JACQUES LAFFITE

Born in 1943, Jacques Laffite entered motor racing as mechanic to his friend Jean-Pierre Jabouille. Laffite began racing in the Formula France series then moved on to F3. He was French F3 champion in 1973 driving a Martini. With BP sponsorship he moved to F2 for 1974 with a March-BMW. His talent was noticed by Frank Williams who signed him for the Williams F1 team halfway through the 1974 season.

Laffite had a single podium place with Williams in 1975 when much more came in F2 where he took the European title. He was also driving for the Autodelta-run Alfa Romeo team in sports-car events. With a Type 33 he took wins at Dijon, Monza and the Nürburgring. Laffite then moved to French team Ligier, which was racing in F1 with the V-12 Matra engine. Some places in 1976 were followed with victory in Sweden in 1977, Laffite scoring his first championship win and also the first for Ligier.

After a win-less 1978 Ligier abandoned the Matra unit and went over to the DFV Cosworth for 1979. This brought Laffite championship wins in Argentina and Brazil and a string of podium places. Ligier went back to the Matra engine in 1981, Laffite scoring wins in Austria and Canada. These were his last championship successes.

Jacques Laffite had two seasons with Williams in 1983 and 1984 before returning to Ligier, newly Renault-powered for 1985 and 1986. After some places it all came to a stop when he was badly hurt in a crash in the British G. P. At the time he had equalled the record for F1 championship appearances, driving in 176 races.

Though Laffite gave up F1, once recovered from his injuries he carried on in touring-car races. He also drove sports-racing cars, carrying on from his early drives for Ligier at Le Mans, where he also appeared for Alpine-Renault and Mirage. In 1995 he raced an Opel in touring-car races and also drove a McLaren F1 GTR in some major events, including Le Mans, showing that he was still on the pace. He then retired from active participation to build a new career as a TV commentator.

Jacques Laffite was an underrated driver who was too often in teams that were having indifferent seasons. With better machinery in F1, as he showed in the best years of Ligier, he could have made a much bigger mark.

---

effect era. Laffite was joined by Patrick Depailler, creating rivalry as each was seen as joint number one.

Laffite won the opening championship rounds in Argentina and Brazil and Depailler won in Spain, but Depailler then hurt himself in a hang-gliding accident and was unfit for the rest of the season. Belgian Jacky Ickx came out of semi-retirement to fill the seat but was off the pace. That no more wins came was a sign of aerodynamic problems, attributable to a move to a new wind tunnel in mid-season. Laffite continued with a hat-trick of third places and, but for a run of retirements at the end of the season, might have been in with a chance of winning the Championship.

The JS11 was revised to become the JS15 in 1980, when Laffite was joined by Didier Pironi who had been making his mark in the Tyrrell team. Pironi paid his way by winning the Belgian G. P. at Zolder while Laffite scored in the German G. P. at Hockenheim. The pair picked up a clutch of places, at the end of the season placing Ligier second in the Constructors' Championship.

Amongst convoluted motor-industry amalgamations and takeovers during the 1970s and 1980s, Chrysler had sold its Simca interest to Peugeot in 1978. This included the earlier Talbot name which had come from the old STD

combine via Rootes, which had been bought earlier by Chrysler. Included in Simca's assets was not only the old Talbot-Lago company but also Matra Sports, so in 1979 Matra came into the orbit of Peugeot, renamed Talbot-Peugeot.

Talbot-Peugeot realised the value of race success to the enhancement of a brand, a polishing desperately needed by the Talbot marque during its relaunch throughout Europe. Thus Talbot-Peugeot teamed up with Ligier, which would use the Matra engine again in 1981. The V-12 was substantially uprated and put in a new JS17.

The championship season began with rows about skirts and ground effects. Once the disputes had been settled the strictly legal Ligiers became very competitive; Laffite won in Austria and Canada and picked up a string of seconds and thirds. Finishing fourth in a close Championship, Laffite had been a hot contender right up to the end of the season. It was less good in 1982; Laffite being joined by American Eddie Cheever in a new JS19, but the results were disappointing. At the end of the season Laffite went off to the Williams team.

Results were worse still in 1983. The Matra deal came to an end so the team went back to the DFV V-8. The drivers were now Jean-Paul Jarier and Brazilian Raul

Jacques Laffite drove the Ligier-Matra JS5 at the 1976 Monaco Grand Prix.

LIGIER

The V-12 Matra engine was an ambitious effort.

In 1988, when a British Judd V-8 was used, Ligier suffered the humiliation of failure to qualify in some races. It was the same tale in 1989 and 1990, using the 3.5-litre Cosworth DFR. A Lamborghini V-12 went into the JS35 for 1991, which resulted in another season without points. Renault supplied its powerful V-10 for 1992, when there was a slight improvement as the Ligiers became mid-field runners instead of tail-enders.

Guy Ligier had virtually severed his contacts with the team in 1992, selling most of his interest to Cyril de Rouvre. Ligier was now managed by the Briton Tom Walkinshaw. British drivers Martin Brundle and Mark Blundell, signed for 1993, picked up three podium finishes. The V-10 Renault was still used in 1994, delivering a surprising 2-3 in the German G. P. after many rivals were eliminated in a multiple accident.

A new power unit, the Honda-based Mugen V-10, went into the Ligiers in 1995 when the best result was a second place by Frenchman Olivier Panis in the Australian G. P., the last race of the season. There was to be one final flash of glory. In a wet 1996 Monaco G. P. where nearly all the field dropped out, Ligier-mounted Panis came through to an unexpected victory.

Monaco was the last Ligier success. At the end of 1996 the team was sold to

Boesel, who came with welcome sponsorship backing. It was no use. The DFV was now outclassed as rival teams had moved on to turbocharged 1.5-litre engines and so the pair scored no championship points.

Helping out a fellow French outfit Renault, now back in Grand Prix racing, supplied its V-6 turbocharged 1,500 cc engine to Ligier in 1984. It made little difference as there was a string of retirements. Laffite rejoined the team in 1985. This brought a slight improvement with a second place and two thirds using the Renault engine in the JS27.

Hopes were high for 1986, but after some good early results Jacques Laffite was badly injured in a multiple crash in the British G. P. and gave up Formula 1 racing. After that it was downhill. Ligier did a deal with Alfa Romeo to supply engines for 1987, but after the engine was disparaged by his new lead driver, René Arnoux, in a test session, that deal was off. The team had to convert its JS29, designed for the Alfa engine, to fit a BMW turbo unit—a hopeless marriage.

four-times World Champion Alain Prost. Renamed 'Prost', the cars used Honda engines in 1997, then moved on to Peugeot V-10s in 1998, 1999 and 2000. The only notable place was a second by Panis in the 1997 Spanish G. P. Apart from that there was nothing to show. A move to Ferrari V-10s in 2001 did not stop the rot. Prost's team was in severe financial trouble, the Gauloises tobacco sponsorship having gone at the end of 2000. At the end of the 2001 season the Prost team was put into liquidation.

Ligier nearly made it to the top. The team carried the French blue valiantly after the withdrawal of Matra. Like so many teams in F1, however, once the downward spiral began it was impossible to stop. The outcome was inevitable.

1975 LIGIER JS5

ITS HUGE AIR INTAKE MADE THE 1976 LIGIER JS5, WITH ITS 3.0–LITRE MATRA ENGINE, DISTINCTIVE ON THE CIRCUITS. A FORMULA 1 RULE
CHANGE OUTLAWED THE TALL AIRBOX AFTER THE EARLY CHAMPIONSHIP ROUNDS IN THE 1976 SEASON.

The 1977 Ligier-Matra JS7.

**Jacques Laffite piloted the Ligier-DFV
Ford JS11 in the 1979 Monaco Grand Prix.**

CHAPTER 17

Renault Resurgence

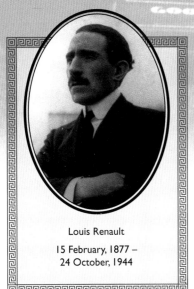

Louis Renault

15 February, 1877 –
24 October, 1944

AFTER 1935's Monte Carlo Rally victory no more major motor-sporting participation came from Renault before World War 2. The war years were bad ones for Renault. Louis Renault felt he had a responsibility to his workers, so tried to keep the Billancourt factory running as normally as possible. Inevitably he was forced to make lorries for the German occupiers.

After Paris was liberated in August 1944, Louis Renault was arrested and charged with collaboration. At the time of his arrest he was severely beaten by communists working in the factory and died soon afterward, probably as a result of his injuries. In February 1945 the Renault company was nationalised, almost certainly for political reasons although Louis Renault's collaboration was cited as justification.

During the war a small rear-engined saloon was developed which appeared in 1946 as the '750' or 'Quatre Chevaux'. The Renault 750 ran at Le Mans in 1949, beginning appearances which continued until 1955. There were class wins in the Mille Miglia and many rally successes. Renault was technically ambitious, building a gas-turbine record car, the 'Etoile Filante', in 1956, designed by none other than the evergreen Albert Lory.

In 1955 Jean Redélé, who had been an active Renault driver, formed a company based in Dieppe, Alpine, to make sporting cars based on Renault parts. A range of neat GT coupés appeared. After Amédée Gordini closed down his team in 1957 he worked for Renault and Alpine developing the production-based engines which gave the Alpines many successes, especially in rallies. Alpines ran at Le Mans from 1963 and won the Index of Energy prize in 1964. During these years René Bonnet was also making Renault-based cars, one of his machines winning the Energy Index at Le Mans in 1963.

In 1965 Alpine entered Formula 2 and 3 with cars using Renault-based engines, but gained little success. A parallel Alpine sports-racing car effort produced the 1,000 cc and 1,200 cc A210, which gained some successes between 1964 and 1969. These were joined in 1967 by the A220 powered by a 3.0-litre V-8 from the workshops of Amédée Gordini. Although this was not fast enough to challenge the established leaders, an A210 fitted with the V-8 gained third place in the 1968 Monza 1,000 km. The racing programme was shelved in 1969, activity then concentrating on rallying.

In 1971 Alpine, although still independent, became the competition department of Renault. A design team headed by François Castaing began work on a 2.0-litre V-6 intended to contest the European 2.0-litre sports-car Championship. Nothing was achieved in 1973 but in 1974

The Renault 'Etoile Filante' set a world record for gas-turbine cars in 1956 at 192.50 mph (309.73 km/h).

the A441 Renault-Alpine won the Championship, taking all seven rounds.

The A441 grew up the next year when a turbocharger was fitted to the V-6 engine, becoming the A442. This won the Mugello 1,000 km, a round of the World Manufacturers' Championship, driven by Jabouille and Larrousse. The A442 failed to gain any more wins in 1975, though the A441 continued to pick up places amongst the 2.0-litre runners.

After Alpine was absorbed by Renault at the beginning of 1976, serious work began with the aim of a win at Le Mans. Two cars eliminated each other in a crash at the Nürburgring, but there was a second place in the Monza Four Hours. Disappointment followed at Le Mans. A single car, now predominantly Renault yellow rather than French blue, led the race before dropping out during the night. There was slight consolation at the end of the season with a second and third in the Dijon 500 km.

Total commitment went into Le Mans in 1977. It was the only race which Renault entered. Observers noted it was almost a military operation, even dwarfing the Mercedes-Benz onslaughts of earlier years. Four A442s ran and by early evening were placed 1-2-3. It seemed a Renault win was inevitable, but then the team fell apart with engine failures, the last with just two hours to go.

A humiliated Renault team picked up the bits and started work for 1978, when Le Mans was again the only race. Much work was done on the aerodynamics of the A442s which had greatly extended tails. As before four cars started and early in the race were running 1-2-3. Then mechanical problems began. Two dropped out but the other pair kept going. Didier Pironi and Jean-Pierre Jaussaud came home as the winners with the sister Renault fourth. The huge investment had finally paid off. Afterward the winning car and its drivers paraded triumphantly along the Champs Elysées in Paris. Renault announced that its aim had been achieved and the company would be withdrawing from endurance racing.

Not quite every Renault effort had gone into the sports-racers. In 1976 Renault's racers realised that their turbocharged V-6 engine might make an F1 unit. At that time the Grand Prix formula was for 3.0 litres unsupercharged and 1.5 litres supercharged. Although this seemed to give the advantage to the blown engine—and was much speculated about when the rules were launched in 1966—none of the participants had given a supercharged unit much thought. Apart from an unsuccessful two-car effort by DB with Roots-blown 746 cc engines at Pau in 1955, no pressure-induction car had run in F1 since 1953. Renault were about to become pioneers.

A small team was briefed to start work on an F1 project. A prototype F1 car was built in the Dieppe workshops. Michelin offered substantial support and a suitable engine was prepared. After the takeover of Alpine, work was transferred to Renault-Gordini at Viry-Châtillon, south of Paris. The RS01 made its race debut at Silverstone in July 1977, driven by Jean-Pierre Jabouille. Finished in a yellow, white and blue livery, it failed to finish and there were three more retirements before the end of the season.

Though development continued in 1978, there were no great results. Initially the F1 opposition didn't take the venture too seriously, dubbing Renault's racer the 'tea kettle' for its frequent steaming blow-ups. Rival design departments began to think furiously, though, when it was seen that the RS01 was noticeably quicker than the rest in a straight line.

Two new RS10s with ground-effect skirts and underbodies were built for 1979. René Arnoux joined Jabouille. After a disappointing start to the season a magnificent result came, appropriately in the French G. P. at Dijon-Prenois. The two RS10s were on the front row of the grid. Jabouille won and Arnoux was third. It was the first Renault Grand Prix victory since the initial win in 1906. Now a major force in F1, Renault had shown the other teams that the future was turbocharged.

For 1980 the RE20 appeared, the 'E' representing Elf, a major sponsor and indeed a magnificent backer of French racing in general. Once again the cars were faster than the opposition but unreliable. Arnoux began the season with wins in Brazil and South Africa, followed by a long run of retirements and a wait of nearly six months before Jabouille won the Austrian G. P.

There was sadness in the French motor-racing world when Patrick Depailler, who had been a key driver for Ligier and a member of Renault's sports-car team, was killed when testing at the Österreichring before the Austrian G. P. The season ended on a down-note for Renault when Jabouille had a bad crash during the Canadian G. P., suffering severe leg fractures after a front wishbone broke.

An unfit Jabouille left Renault and Alain Prost was signed for 1981. Prost was a graduate of Formula Renault, a nursery class for budding drivers where he had shone. He had started in F1 with McLaren in 1980 with little success, but that would soon change. Prost and Arnoux began the

This Alpine-Renault A110 competed in the 1965 Sebring 12 Hours.

season with a lengthened RE20, the RE20B. Uncertain F1 regulations early in 1981 concerning sliding skirts caused problems, but when the controversy was resolved former Ligier designer Michel Tétu produced the RE30 which was lighter and had improved suspension. The cast-iron cylinder block of the V-6 engine was replaced with an aluminium counterpart.

The first half of the season was dismal, Arnoux even failing to qualify in Belgium. It all came good in the French G. P. at Dijon however. The race was stopped as the course was flooded by a downpour at half-distance, but after a restart Prost was the winner, his first victory in what was to be a remarkable career. He went on to take wins in the Dutch and Italian G. P.s. The season ended with Renault taking a promising third place in the Constructors' Championship.

The RE30 was mildly improved for 1982. Prost made a brilliant start with wins in South Africa and Brazil but then the effort faded with a string of retirements. There was great relief for Renault when Arnoux and Prost came first and second in the crucial French G. P. at Paul Ricard. Arnoux followed this up with a win at Monza, so Renault were third in the Constructors' Championship again.

For 1983 the F1 regulations were changed once more, requiring that the undersides of the cars should be flat to reduce escalating downforce. Tétu designed the RE40, using carbon-composite construction which had previously been rejected by the Renault management on safety grounds. Arnoux had gone to Ferrari and so Prost was joined by American Eddie Cheever.

Prost had a good season with wins in the French, Belgian, British and Austrian G. P.s. Cheever backed him up with one second and three third places. A turbocharger failure in the last Championship round in South Africa cost Prost the Drivers' Championship by a single point, while Renault was runner-up in the Constructors' Championship.

After Renault had shown the way, the turbocharged engine was now almost standard equipment in F1. Captured at a vulnerable moment by McLaren's Ron Dennis after his South African disappointment at the end of 1983, Prost left Renault and for 1984 went back to

McLaren who offered him a Porsche-designed engine. He was replaced by Patrick Tambay, who came from Ferrari, while Cheever's place was taken by Briton Derek Warwick.

The Orwellian year 1984 had a promising start as Warwick with the new RE50 led in Brazil until a front wishbone broke. After that it was a season of disappointment. There were three second places but neither Warwick nor Tambay could threaten to win a race. The Renault competition department had split; engine development and preparation remained at Viry-Châtillon while chassis construction and preparation was moved to Evry.

These moves plus managerial upsets in search of economies caused problems. Gérard Larrousse, the Renault team manager, left to go to Ligier, taking Michel Tétu with him and leaving behind a half-finished design of the RE60. Though its V-6 engine was substantially redesigned the RE60 was unsatisfactory and after two third places at the beginning of the 1985 season it all fell apart. Renault announced it was withdrawing from F1. By the end of the season Tambay and Warwick were barely also-rans.

The Renault A442B was victorious at Le Mans in 1978.

Jean-Pierre Jabouille won the 1979 French
Grand Prix at Dijon in the Renault RS11 —
the first Renault F1 win but not the company's
first Grand Prix victory.

Alain Prost drove the Renault RS30B in the
1982 British Grand Prix at Brands Hatch.

ALAIN PROST

Established in the 1960s to encourage new driving talent, Formula France and Formula Renault have produced several generations of fine drivers. The shining star has been Alain Prost. Like his bitter rival Ayrton Senna and Britain's Lewis Hamilton, Prost served his apprenticeship in go-karting. Born in the Loire in 1955, he started karting at 15. In 1975 he won the French senior karting championship and graduated to Formula Renault where he was champion in 1976, then taking the Super Renault title in 1977. The next stage was F3. With a Martini he carried off the French and European titles in 1979.

Such talent attracted the attention of F1 teams. Prost was offered a contract by McLaren in 1980. It was a mildly disappointing season with some points placings punctuated by accidents. Renault had been keeping an eye on their favourite son, who joined the French team for the 1981 season. Three championship triumphs included—perhaps most satisfyingly—his first win in the French G.P., a victory by a Frenchman in a French car. Prost stayed with Renault in 1982 and 1983 to notch up another six wins.

The World Championship seemed in Prost's grasp in 1983, but a turbo failure in the last round in South Africa demoted him to second place. This disappointment left him open to an approach from McLaren, whom he rejoined for 1984. It was a richly rewarding move. McLaren was using the Porsche-designed TAG turbo unit with which Prost and his team-mate Niki Lauda dominated the season. Prost won seven championship rounds and Lauda won five, taking the title from Prost by a mere half point. This was a consequence of Prost's win at Monaco only receiving half points after the race was stopped by heavy rain.

In 1985 Prost couldn't be denied. He won five rounds, took podium places in most of the other races and was World Champion. Going was much tougher in 1986. Though his McLaren-TAG was no longer dominant, driving brilliance, four wins and a clutch of places took Prost to his second World Championship. After the glories of the two previous seasons

1987 was a relatively lean year. McLaren was fighting to stay competitive, Prost taking only three championship wins.

Ayrton Senna joined McLaren in 1988, bringing the Honda turbo engine with him. This put McLaren right at the top again and the team won 15 of the 16 championship rounds. An intense rivalry began between Prost and Senna. Senna won eight rounds and Prost seven, the title going to Senna by three points.

The pair stayed with McLaren in 1989. Once again the McLaren Honda was dominant but the rivalry between the drivers became more heated. It came to a head in the penultimate championship round in Japan. Prost and Senna collided while fighting for the lead amid accusations that each had pushed the other off. Prost took the World Championship then left McLaren, aggrieved that he was not being accorded undisputed number one status.

Like so many drivers Prost took the road to Maranello and joined Ferrari. He took five wins in 1990 and might have won the championship again but for another collision with Senna in Japan. In 1991 Ferrari was off the pace and Prost could only pick up places. Disillusioned, he took a year off. He was back again in 1993, teaming with the French Renault engines being used by Williams. It was another magnificent season. Prost won seven rounds and won his fourth World Championship. At the end of 1993 he announced his retirement. Until Michael Schumacher surpassed his record Prost was the most successful driver in Formula 1.

Alain Prost became a team owner when he acquired the Ligier team in 1997. It did not prosper and the Prost team withdrew from F1 in 2002 with little to show for its effort and expenditure. Prost was a driver who not only had skills in abundance but also—unlike many of his rivals—applied a high degree of intelligence to his racing. 'The Professor', as he was aptly known, stood shoulder to shoulder with the great French-blue heroes of the past.

Other frustrations troubled Renault. In 1983 a deal had been made to supply the V-6 engine to Team Lotus. This went into the Lotus 93T and 94T, both designed by Gérard Decarouge, who had moved on from Ligier to Lotus. Elio de Angelis and Nigel Mansell had little success using the V-6 in 1983. There was an improved Lotus 94T in 1984. While unable to win a Championship round, de Angelis picked up several seconds and thirds. His results were good enough to give him third place in the Championship and also to place Lotus third amongst the constructors. Renault, ironically, could only manage fifth place.

For 1985 Lotus signed a promising Brazilian newcomer, Ayrton Senna, who was showing the brilliance that would make him one of the all-time greats. Ducarouge produced the Lotus 97T and Senna used it to score his first Championship victory in Portugal and went on to win in Belgium, while de Angelis won in San Marino.

While Renault was no longer a direct participant in F1, its redesigned V-6 engine, the EF.15, remained competitive. Bernard Dudot, who had worked with Castaing on the original V-6, had produced a new cylinder block with more-over-square dimensions that would take a higher turbo boost pressure. Engine manufacture and development continued, Dudot devising a remarkable system of valve closure operated by a supply of nitrogen gas operating on a piston atop the valve stem. This pneumatic system resulted in lighter valve gear, allowing higher engine revolutions while also reducing engine height and weight.

Renault engines supplied direct to Lotus for the 1986 season were giving a remarkable output of 1,100 bhp for qualifying. The engines also went to Ligier and Tyrrell through Mechachrome, a subcontractor. Neither Ligier nor Tyrrell made any showing but Senna had wins in Spain and the USA, together with four second places. At the end of the season Senna, who carried a lot of sponsorship, persuaded Lotus that there was a better deal to be had with Honda. The Renault contract, which still had a year to run, was abandoned. Renault decided to have a short break and pulled out of F1 engine supply. They would soon return.

The Renault 1.5-litre turbo engine powered the RS01.

Ayrton Senna competed with the Lotus-Renault 97T at Monaco in 1985.

CHAPTER 18

The Lion of Peugeot Roars again

DURING the erratic phase in which motor racing resumed in 1946, Charles de Cortanze made a reappearance. He had been one of the drivers in the successful Darl'Mat 302/402 sports Peugeots which had made a good showing at Le Mans in 1937 and 1938. He brought out one of the 302/402s, replacing its aerodynamic body with neat racing coachwork. Its 2.0-litre engine made the car eligible for the *Voiturette* class, which became Formula 2, in 1947.

De Cortanze was a regular competitor in 1946 and 1947, battling with the Simca-Gordini team and picking up several places. When Formula 2 became more serious in 1948, with the arrival of Ferrari, De Cortanze withdrew. In November 1947 an 1,100 cc Peugeot 202 aerodynamic coupé appeared at Montlhéry. This had been devised by Darl'mat, which was still producing tuned Peugeots. It took international class records up to 12 hours.

The first post-war production model to come from Peugeot was the 1,290 cc 203 saloon. A 203 was tuned by a Paris engineer, Alexis Constantin, who fitted a Roots-type supercharger. This ran at Le Mans in 1952 and 1953 but without success. Constantin was back at Le Mans in 1954 and 1955 with a sports-racing car using 203 parts, but failed to finish in either year.

Maurice Dubois, a Peugeot agent in Argenteuil, commissioned the Italian constructor Enrico Nardi to make a lightweight chassis to take 203 components. It had an attractive coupé body. Driven by Fernand Sigrand and co-driver Celerier, it won the 1954 24-hour Bol d'Or at Montlhéry. The 203 saloon took a class place in the 1955 Mille Miglia, but after that Peugeot faded away on the circuits.

The 1,600 cc Peugeot 404 appeared in 1960. In 1963 a 404 ran in the East Africa Safari Rally. At that time it was the toughest rally in the world, run over tracks and unmade roads through the African bush. The winning 404 was driven by Kenyan drivers Nick Norwicki and Paddy Cliff. There was another 404 win in the 1967 Safari, when the victorious drivers were Tanzanians Bert Shankland and Cliff Rothwell.

Shankland and Rothwell won again in 1967, then Norwicki and Cliff were back to take the 1968 event. The Safari had achieved a huge status and all the major rally teams were competing by the 1970s. The 404 was replaced by the 504, an equally rugged car, in 1968. A 504 driven by the Swedish pair Ove Anderson and Arne Hertz won the 1975 Safari.

The cost of developing new production models had soared, so in the early 1970s Peugeot collaborated with

Renault and ultimately Volvo in the development and manufacture of a V-6 2.6-litre engine, which was built at Douvrin near Lens. A V-6 in a coupé version of the 504 won the 1978 Safari, driven by Jean-Pierre Nicholas and Jean-Claude Lefébre.

After his split with René Bonnet, Charles Deutsch continued to make cars in small numbers. His CDs appeared at Le Mans with Panhard engines. Then in 1966 and 1967 he used 204 Peugeot engines, but the cars failed to finish. Soon afterwards Deutsch gave up making CDs

and in the 1970s became Minister of Transport in the French government.

In the late 1960s Michel Meunier and Gérard Welter were working in the Peugeot design office at Garennes-Colombes. To satisfy their motor-racing ambitions in their spare time they designed a sports coupé, the WM, using Peugeot 204 parts. They branched into tuning extras for Peugeots, made in a small factory at Thorigny-sur-Marne.

In 1976 Meunier and Welter designed a light-alloy monocoque rear-engined WM coupé which used state-of-

Based on Peugeot 203 components, the Peugeot MD won the 1954 Bol d'Or at Montlhéry.

Peugeot's 504 gained some notable wins in the East Africa Safari Rally.

the-art aerodynamics. Built by Secateva, a specialist constructor in Thorigny, this used a 2.6-litre V-6 based on the standard Douvrin-made components. It ran at Le Mans in 1976 but retired with a fuel leak. WM was back at Le Mans next year with two cars, one with a turbo-blown V-6, and managed to finish 15th. There were three WMs at Le Mans in 1978, but all retired.

Only concerned with Le Mans, Meunier and Welter had a passion for maximum speed to the exclusion of other factors. Their first minor success came in 1979 when one of the three cars entered won the Le Mans GT Prototype class, although only finishing 14th. The V-6 was uprated in

1980 with twin turbos, which took a WM into fourth place at Le Mans. Later in 1980 a WM ran in the Dijon 1,000 km and might have won but for a turbo failure.

Disaster followed at Le Mans in 1981. Belgian F1 driver Thierry Boutsen crashed a WM at high speed on the Mulsanne Straight. He escaped, but flying debris from the car killed a marshal. The cars were being entered by Secateva, which had greater ambitions in 1982 in the form of a larger racing programme. New monocoques used ground effects. As well as Le Mans, where two cars retired, there were entries at Monza, Silverstone and Spa. At Monza a chance of success was lost by a refuelling error.

The fastest ever: the WM-Peugeot P88 was timed at 251.50 mph (405 km/h) on the Mulsanne Straight during the 1988 Le Mans 24 Hours.

Peugeot's exotic 905 won the 1992 Le Mans 24-Hour race.

The 1983 season saw new monocoques again, but narrower and sleeker, Two cars ran at Le Mans, achieving only a disappointing 16th place.

Development of the WM continued but with little to show save lowly places at Le Mans. In 1988 Denis Mathoit, who prepared the engines, increased capacity to 3.6 litres and on the test-bench saw 950 bhp. Equipped with this unit, the WM failed again in the 24 Hours but set an all-time record. On the Mulsanne Straight Roger Dorchy was timed at 253 mph (409 km/h), the highest speed ever recorded in the race, achieving one of the aims of Welter and Meunier. It is a record unlikely to be broken as the Mulsanne Straight was slowed by chicanes in subsequent years.

The last appearance of WM at Le Mans was in 1989. Meunier gave up, but Welter continued with Peugeot-engined cars, now WRs, using the turbo 2.0-litre L4 and the 3.3-litre V6 ES9J, which ran intermittently at Le Mans until 2006, though without success.

The Douvrin V-6 was the power unit of the Venturi. This appeared in 1984 as a turbo-blown mid-engined coupé made at Coueron, near Nantes, and was intended to be the French answer to the road-going Ferrari. A competition programme was launched which culminated in success for the Venturi 600 LM in 1994. Running in the BPR race series for GT cars, there were wins in the Dijon 4 Hours, the Paris 1,000 kms at Montlhéry and the Spa 4 Hours.

Although eschewing direct racing participation, Peugeot had been active in competition motoring. Appreciating that rally success sold more cars than racing, it mounted an intensive rally programme. Under the guidance of Jean Todt, a former rally driver, a works turbo 205 took the 1985 World Rally Championship with Timo Salonen the Drivers' Champion. These successes were repeated in 1986 when the 205 was the favoured car again

and Juha Kankkunen the top driver.

Doubtless urged by the ambitious Todt, Peugeot now made an official return to the racing circuits after a break of over 60 years. In 1988 the Peugeot Talbot Sport department at Velizy-Villacoublay, the former home of Matra Sport, reverberated again to the scream of a racing engine. A 3.5-litre V-10 was developed which went into a carbon-fibre monocoque hull designed by André de Cortanze and built by the aircraft manufacturer Dassault. This car, the Peugeot 905, entered the last two rounds of the 1990 World Sports-Car Championship but failed to finish.

A major assault on the World Sports Car Championship was launched in 1991. F1 drivers Keke Rosberg, Yannick Dalmas, Phillipe Alliot and Mauro Baldi were signed. Success began with a win at Suzuka in Japan, where a 905 came first after the favoured Jaguars dropped out. Subsequent setbacks included failures at Le Mans and the Nürburgring. Rapid work was done. For the vital home round at Magny-Cours the 905B appeared with improved aerodynamics and a more powerful engine. This paid off with first and second places. The 905Bs then crossed the Atlantic to Mexico for the penultimate points-scoring round and scored another 1-2. At the end of the season Peugeot was in second place in the championship.

The 1992 Championship drew a thin entry from manufacturers. Peugeot continued to develop its 905B and produced a more advanced Evo2 version at the end of the season. Rosberg was replaced by Derek Warwick in the

JEAN TODT

Jean Todt was born in 1946 at Pierrefort in the Auvergne, the son of a doctor. He began a motor-sporting career in club rallying and gradually moved on to the international scene. He found his talents were suited as a co-driver and partnered many of the leading rally drivers in the 1970s including Rauno Aaltonen and Ove Anderson.

When Peugeot purchased Chrysler France's interests in 1979, the name of Talbot was revived and Todt became a member of the Talbot Sunbeam Lotus team in 1979. Paired with Guy Frequelin, they were a successful combination. Many World Rally Championship placings followed plus one win in Argentina in 1981. Their 1981 results took them to runner-up place in the championship.

At the end of 1981 Todt retired from active rallying and took on the task of turning the Peugeot 205 into a top-line rally car. Using the Turbo 16 version Todt developed a formidable car with which Peugeot won the 1985 and 1986 World Rally Championships.

Doubtless encouraged by Todt, Peugeot then decided to go motor-racing again. Todt supervised the design and building of a V-10 engine in the competition department at Velizy-Villacoublay. This went into the advanced Peugeot 905 which appeared on the circuits at the end of 1990. A full World Sports Car Championship season was tackled in 1991 under Todt's management. The prime aim was a Le Mans win, but the cars fell by the wayside. Compensation came with victories at Magny-Cours and in Mexico and Japan.

When the Le Mans effort was renewed in 1992 with the 905B, Todt's efforts were rewarded with victory. This, with other successes, gave Peugeot the World Sports-Car Championship. Every effort was concentrated on Le Mans in 1993. Here again Peugeot, under Todt's management, triumphed. A grateful nation honoured him with appointment as a Chevalier of the Legion d'Honneur.

Jean Todt was feted by the Peugeot drivers after the 1992 Le Mans win.

Todt felt that his V-10 engine was a potential F1 contender but he couldn't persuade Peugeot to take the plunge. Ferrari recognised his talents so he moved to Italy in 1994 to become the team manager of the legendary Prancing Horse. His masterstroke was to sign Michael Schumacher to begin, in 1996, almost a decade of Ferrari domination.

In 2003 Todt became the general manager of Ferrari and from 2006 until 2008 was its CEO. In 2007 he was promoted in the Legion d'Honneur to the rank of Grand Officer. One of the all-time-great racing-team managers, Jean Todt played a major part in Peugeot's successful return to racing.

driver line-up. Fading brakes saw the 905Bs beaten by a Toyota at Monza, but it was back to the winner's circle in the points round at Silverstone. Le Mans was the main prize and it all went to plan. Dalmas, Warwick and Mark Blundell took the 905B to a comfortable victory and the other 905B was third. Further wins followed at Donington, Suzuka and Magny-Cours, so Peugeot were impressive champions.

A lack of entries and disputes about regulations saw the championship abandoned in 1993. Peugeot concentrated solely on Le Mans. The Toyotas led in the early hours of the 1993 race but hit problems and the 905Bs moved up into the three leading places. The Japanese challenge faded to leave a Peugeot 1-2-3, with Eric Hélary, Christophe Bouchut and Geoffrey Brabham in the winning car. There

was nothing more to prove, so Peugeot announced that it would be pulling out of sports-car racing at the end of 1993.

Having conquered the sports-car world, Peugeot's Jean Todt now had higher aspirations. He wanted to enter F1, for which the V-10 engine seemed to need little development to create a suitable unit, but Peugeot management said '*Non*'. Todt walked out to join Ferrari, where he masterminded a remarkable run of success.

Although no direct Peugeot entry in F1 eventuated, there was a change of policy. Both the developed V-10 and sponsorship were supplied to McLaren in 1994, but it was an unhappy marriage and McLaren abandoned Peugeot for Mercedes-Benz at the end of the season. The V-10 was then supplied to the Jordan team for the 1995, 1996 and

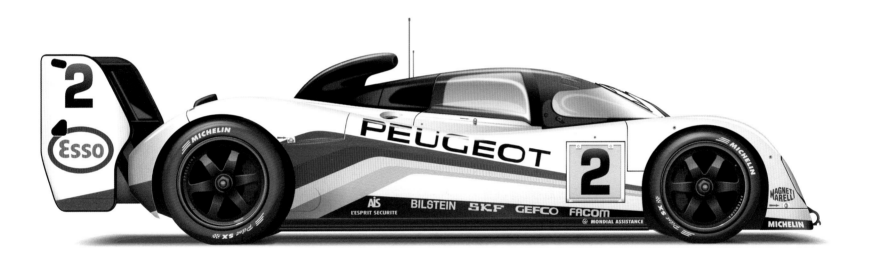

1992 PEUGEOT 905B

POWERED BY A 3.5-LITRE V-10 ENGINE, THE PEUGEOT 905B SCORED A NOTABLE WIN IN THE 1992 LE MANS 24-HOUR RACE, DRIVEN BY
DEREK WARWICK, YANNICK DALMAS AND MARK BLUNDELL. IT ALSO GAINED THE 1992 WORLD SPORTS-CAR CHAMPIONSHIP.

Peugeot's V-10 engine was a disappointment in F1.

Top right: Seen during testing before the 2008 Le Mans 24-Hour race, the Peugeot 908.

Right: Peugeot's 908 won the 2008 Le Mans Series round at Catalunya.

1997 seasons, when results were equally poor. The Prost team took over the V-10 for three seasons, but it was the same story and Peugeot disappeared from the F1 world at the end of 2000.

Peugeot went back to rallying. The 206 won the World Rally Championship for manufacturers in 2000, 2001 and 2002, while the Finnish driver Marcus Grönholm was the Drivers' Champion in 2000 and 2002.

The lure of the circuits and the need for technical advances brought Peugeot back to circuit racing in the 21st Century. Development of the 908 5.5-litre V-12 turbo-diesel began in 2006 based on a carbon-fibre monocoque chassis. It was entered for the Le Mans Series Championship in 2007 and won its first race, the Monza 1,000 km. It was beaten at Le Mans in the 24 Hours by an Audi but took second place, coming back to gain wins at Valencia, the Nürburgring, Spa, Silverstone and in Brazil. These impressive results gained the Le Mans Series Championship.

Peugeot came back with its 908 for the 2008 season. Once again Audi took the biggest prize of all, beating the 908s into second, third and fourth place in the coveted Le Mans 24 Hours. There was a run of Peugeot successes in the Le Mans Series Championship with victory for the 908 at Catalunya, Monza, Spa and the Nürburgring. The championship was awarded to the best individual car, but as the results were split amongst the Peugeot team, Audi took the prize.

Peugeot have carried the blue in the highest traditions of French racing for over a century. The Peugeot lion will persevere. Seeking technical advances, a hybrid electric 908 is planned to compete on the world's circuits in 2009.

CHAPTER 19

Renault–Resurgence Resumed

The Benetton-Renault B195 took Michael Schumacher to the 1995 World Drivers' Championship title.

CONCERNED about the domination of costly turbo engines, for 1987 the FIA admitted unblown engines of 3.5 instead of 3.0 litres to race against the turbocharged 1,500 cc machines. At the end of the 1988 season the turbo engines were banned. This roused Renault's interest. Bernard Dudot was directed to start work on a 3.5-litre unit. He produced a V-10 engine with a 67-degree vee, the RS01, for which an eager customer appeared.

The Williams team had been racing with Honda engines, but after resisting Honda's demands to nominate a Japanese driver for the team, its engine supply had been cut off. After Williams was forced to use unsatisfactory Judd engines for the 1988 season, the Renault V-10 was a welcome lifeline. Patrick Head, the Williams designer, produced the FW12, tailored for the V-10.

From the beginning of the 1989 season Williams drivers Ricardo Patrese and Thierry Boutsen were picking up places. The Franco-Britannic effort came good in Canada where Boutsen and Patrese scored a one-two. There was another win for Boutsen in the last Championship round in Australia. The results took Williams to second place in the Constructors' Championship; a success which owed much to Renault.

The 1990 season saw a savage battle between the Ferrari of Alain Prost and the McLaren-Honda of Ayrton Senna. Their pace left the other teams breathless. Dudot's redesigned V-10 became the RS2, which went into the Williams FW13. The combination enabled Patrese to win the St Marino G. P. at Imola and Boutsen was successful in Hungary. Boutsen departed at the end of 1990 and Patrese was joined in the Williams team by Nigel Mansell.

Damon Hill was pictured on his way to winning the 1996 Drivers' Championship in the Williams-Renault FW18.

The original RS01 had been intended as a proprietary engine for sale to any customer, but Dudot now worked closely with Williams. His RS3 for 1991 was designed to suit the needs of the Williams team and its new FW14. It paid off. Mansell gained a hat-trick of wins in the French, British and German G. P.s and also took the Italian and Spanish races while Patrese scored in Mexico and Portugal. Williams and Renault were second in the Constructors' Championship, just pipped by the brilliance of Senna and some transmission troubles early in the season.

Nineteen ninety-two was Williams's year. With the V-10—now the RS4—at its peak Mansell dominated the Drivers' Championship. He set a new record by winning nine rounds while Patrese scored one win and Williams, hugely assisted by Renault, was the Constructors' Champion. Mansell left Williams to try his luck in the USA Indy Championship, so Alain Prost was signed for 1993. Prost followed on where Mansell had left off. He won seven championship rounds and once again Williams was the Constructor's Champion. With a French driver and a French engine, there was understandable pride in the Octagon.

It looked set for yet another tour de force in 1994 as Williams signed double World Champion Ayrton Senna in place of Prost. Senna was supported by Damon Hill, son of former World Champion Graham Hill. It all went tragically wrong when Senna was killed at Imola. Hill soldiered on bravely and won five championship rounds, ending the season as runner-up to the new rising star, Michael Schumacher. Mansell returned to the team for a valedictory race and won in Australia.

In Britain the Toleman team had arrived in F1 in 1981. It was a small and tightly financed outfit using Hart turbo engines. Toleman struggled until 1986 when the team was bought by Italian clothing magnate Luciano Benetton. With Benetton's funds and the skills of designer Rory Byrne the team gradually prospered. Appointed as team manager, Flavio Briatore recruited a promising newcomer, Michael Schumacher. It was a Benetton, powered by a Cosworth-built Ford-Zetec V-8, that took Schumacher to the 1994 Drivers' Championship.

For 1995 the F1 rulemakers reverted to a 3.0-litre capacity limit. The V-10 was reworked at the Viry-Châtillon factory, Briatore making an agreement with Renault to supply the V-10 engine to the Benetton team. The unit was identical to that being used by Williams. Aided by the brilliance of Schumacher, Benetton made better use of the V-10 than Williams during the 1995 season.

An indication of the supremacy of the V-10 was that only one points-scoring round in the 1995 season was won by a car not using the Renault unit. Schumacher was champion driver and Benetton the champion constructor. Damon Hill and Williams were the respective runners-up in the Drivers' and Constructors' Championships.

With Schumacher departing to Ferrari, Williams supplanted Benetton as the Renault favourite in 1996. The V-10 was still being supplied to Benetton but the Williams team had the better results. It was still Renault engines

100% RENAULT

The 2002 Renault F1 team, left to right: Jarno Trulli, Jenson Button, Flavio Briatore, Patrick Faure and test driver Fernando Alonso. The wide-angle V-10 engine is on the left.

Jenson Button had a disappointing season in the 2002 Renault R22.

RENAULT

FERNANDO ALONSO

Although he is Spanish, many in France would accept Fernando Alonso as an honorary Frenchman. Alonso, the son of a factory mechanic, was born in Oviedo in 1981. His father was a go-kart fanatic. Although having few resources, he built a kart which the young Fernando drove avidly. He started kart racing in 1993 and by 1996 had won the Junior World Cup. He was Spanish champion in 1997 and 1998 and runner-up in the European Championship.

In 1999 Alonso moved up to the cadet class of car racing, Spanish Euro Open Movi Star, driving single-seaters with Nissan engines. He dominated the class and was 1999 champion. He made a slow start in Formula 3000 to which he graduated in 2000, but he won the last race of the series.

Alonso's progress had been noticed by Flavio Briatore, manager of the Renault F1 team, who had negotiated the F3000

drive. Briatore found him a seat in the Minardi F1 team for 2001. Minardis were well off the pace and Alonso had little to show at the end of the season. For 2002 Briatore signed Alonso for Renault but it was a season marking time as he was the team's test driver. Next year, 2003, Fernando Alonso had a full place in the Renault team.

After a string of places, Alonso won his first championship round in Hungary. Despite a new narrow angle V-10 engine, results were disappointing for 2004 which brought no wins for Alonso, only podium places. The big year was 2005. Alonso won seven championship rounds and was World Champion, then the youngest driver to win the title. The F1 rules changed for 2006 when Renault produced a new V-8 engine. This did all that was expected of it, powering Alonso to a second championship title. He had a struggle with Michael Schumacher throughout the season and needed just one point to become World Champion in the last round in Brazil. A third place clinched it.

Perhaps lured by big-money offers, Alonso left Renault and joined McLaren for the 2007 season where his team-mate was rookie Lewis Hamilton. It was soon evident that Hamilton was not a subservient number two. He had the pace and talent to challenge Alonso right from the start of the season. This made it an unhappy year for Alonso, who began to allege that Hamilton was receiving favoured treatment from the McLaren team. Alonso won four championship rounds but could only take third place in the title chase behind runner-up Hamilton. Alonso was also caught up in the allegations of industrial espionage involving McLaren and Ferrari.

In 2008 Fernando Alonso returned to Renault, where he found himself most at home. For most of the season the Renault was unable to match the pace of the front-runners. Then in the last three championship rounds both Alonso and his car were the fastest combination, finishing the season with two wins and a second place. Especially when paired with Renault, Alonso showed that he is one of the finest talents in F1.

it was Renault's first F1 win since 1983. Though Renault finished the 2003 season as fourth in the Constructors' Championship, the F1 world realised that Renault meant business again.

Despite the win and the places gained in 2003, the wide-angle-vee RS22 and RS23 engines were judged unsatisfactory both structurally and as sources of vibration. Bernard Dudot and Briton Rob White, now technical director at Viry-Châtillon, produced a new and more conventional 72-degree V-10 for 2004.

The season began well with a win for Trulli at Monaco but after that—although there were places—results were disappointing. Though Briatore was Trulli's personal manager, after a disappointing performance in the French G.P. at Magny-Cours Briatore accused his fellow Italian of not trying hard enough. Trulli left the Renault team. Jacques Villeneuve was signed for the remaining races of the season but the results did not improve.

Villeneuve went elsewhere in 2005 and Giancarlo Fisichella returned to partner Alonso. Jean-Phillipe Mercier joined Rob White to continue development work on the

new V-10. The season began well when Fisichella won in Australia. Then Alonso got into his stride with a hat-trick of wins in Malaysia, Bahrain and at Imola after fierce struggles with Schumacher. He scored a lucky win in the European G. P. at the Nürburgring when Kimi Räikkönen hit trouble on the last lap.

The North American rounds of the Championship yielded nothing. Alonso had a collision with an unforgiving wall at Montreal. Renault, together with all the Michelin runners, withdrew from the United States G. P. at Indianapolis when the tyres were deemed unsafe for the course. Back in Europe Alonso had wins in the French and German G. P.s. Then a string of second places, followed by a third in Brazil, secured him the World Championship. The Constructors' title still remained open, but Alonso won in Shanghai, the last Championship round, and Renault was also Makes' Champion. It was a magnificent finale for the V-10 and full validation of Briatore's faith in Alonso.

World Championship rules changed in 2006, when 2.5-litre V-8 engines were mandated. The new engine from Viry-Châtillon was a 72-degree V-8 which owed much to the earlier V-10. At Enstone a new chassis, the R26, was built for it. This had an ingenious spring-mounted mass in the nose of the car to reduce vertical vibration and maintain tyre contact with the track.

There was immediate success. Alonso won in Bahrain and Australia while Fisichella was the victor in Malaysia. Alonso followed two second places with a splendid run of wins in the Spanish, Monaco, British and Canadian G. P.s. Then after a second place in France the FIA decreed that the mass-damper system was illegal. It was suggested that it would be permitted in the German G. P. but Renault decided to abandon the system, fearing that any points scored would be disallowed.

After the FIA confirmed the ban a disappointing run of races followed. It seemed likely that Schumacher would take the World Championship, but a burst engine at Suzuka in Japan ended his hopes. By winning the race Alonso secured his second championship. He took second place in the final round in Brazil and that gained a second Constructors' title for Renault.

At the end of 2006 Fernando Alonso left Renault to sign with McLaren, perhaps a surprising move in view of his close connection to Briatore. At the same time Renault's main sponsor, the tobacco company Mild Seven, withdrew in line with the banning of tobacco sponsorship. ING, the Dutch banking group, moved in to fill the gap. An Alonso-free Renault had a poor 2007 season. Heikki Kovalainen had taken Alonso's place but at the end of the year the team had a solitary podium place to show for its efforts. Alonso had an unhappy season at McLaren, where he judged that his putative rookie team-mate, Lewis Hamilton, garnered too many points and too much team attention for his liking.

Alonso rejoined Renault for 2008, where his new team-mate was Nelson Piquet, the son of a former World Champion. For the early part of 2008 the Renault team had little to show and it threatened to be a repeat of 2007. Then in the latter part of the year both Alonso and the team found greatly improved form. Alonso ran away from the field in Singapore and Japan to score the first Renault wins for two years. He finished the season with a strong second place in Brazil.

Renault faced the 2009 season with a positive approach to podium placings. Although the team is based in England where much construction is done, the spirit of the blue and yellow Renaults is—as the team likes to say—100% French. Its cars carry the national honour—and are finding the glory—in the true tradition of French Racing Blue.

Finn Heikki Kovalainen raced the 2007 Renault RS27.

CHAPTER 20

7 Les Autres

THROUGHOUT the saga of French Racing Blue many names have become immortal legends. Others have disappeared without trace. Still others had brief moments of minor glory before departing from the sporting arena either broke or all too aware that competition participation wasn't delivering hoped-for rewards.

After the French G. P. was established in 1906 it became a magnet for aspiring manufacturers. However few would now recall Porthos or Vulpes on a list of Grand Prix participants. Both were small firms in Paris. Neither found Grand Prix glory; nor did they survive World War 1.

Already an industry leader, France was in the forefront of the huge boom in motoring in the years after World War 1. The cyclecar, small, spidery and often with a twin-cylinder air-cooled engine, came to the fore as cheap motoring for the younger enthusiast.

Salmson, a Paris engineering company, flourished during the war by making aircraft parts. Wanting to move into the cyclecar market, Salmson obtained a licence in 1919 to make the GN—a leading British cyclecar—at its Billancourt factory. The project prospered with Salmson-built GNs even supplied to the Paris police.

To overcome the GN's limitations engineer Emil Petit was engaged by Salmson to design a four-cylinder engine. His 1,100 cc twin-cam unit set Salmson on the road to sporting success. The first major win was the 1921 French Cyclecar G. P., after which Salmsons dominated the 1,100 cc class, gaining victories all over Europe including a class win in the first Le Mans 24-Hour race in 1923.

Petit's design was developed into a pure supercharged racing machine which became known as the San Sebastian model after a major win on the Spanish circuit. In 1927 Petit produced an advanced eight-cylinder 1,100 cc engine which was virtually a miniature Grand Prix unit, but it was not fully developed. Salmson gradually faded from the racing world. It enjoyed a slight sporting revival after World War 2 with unsuccessful entries at Le Mans and minor rally wins, but car production ended in 1957 when Renault took over the small factory.

While Petit was refining the GN at Billancourt, a few miles away at St Denis the Amilcar was being developed. The brainchild of Emil Akar and Joseph Lamy, whose surnames contributed to the brand name, the first Amilcar appeared in 1922. Designed by Edmond Moyet, it had a 1,000 cc side-valve engine. Soon developed into a small sports car, it quickly caught the fancy of French sporting

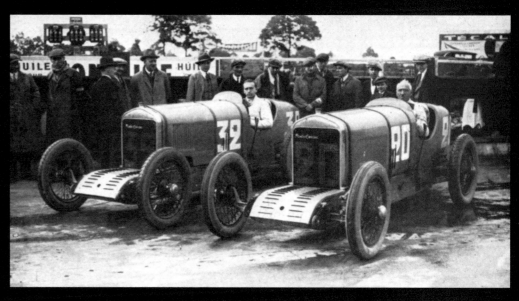

The first Ford-based Montiers competed at Montlhéry in 1927.

The 1.1-litre Amilcar CGS gave many French drivers in the 1920s their first taste of competition.

AMILCAR

René Lebegue, in his Type 135 Delahaye, performed the deciding driving test en route to winning the 1937 Monte Carlo Rally.

drastically. Starting points became more remote and a marking differential was introduced for the more difficult routes. In 1925 a short mountain stage was instituted in the Alpes Maritimes before the competitors reached Monte Carlo.

As cars improved and were better able to cope with the road conditions, driving tests were added in the 1930s to be performed by arrivals at Monte Carlo to determine the winner. When the Monte was revived again after World War 2 a much tougher stage, run during the night in the Alpes Maritimes, became an additional means of winnowing out the winner.

In the immediate post-war years the glamour of the demanding rally attracted vast media publicity. Wins by Hotchkiss in 1949 and 1950 breathed a few extra years of life into an ailing marque. Fields grew in size until a record 440 was reached in 1953. The publicity drew entries from most major manufacturers, making it harder for French companies to obtain a coveted win.

The nature of the event changed in the 1960s. The large numbers of amateur teams which enjoyed the Monte's challenges disappeared

MONTE CARLO RALLY

Although it is organised in the Principality of Monaco, most Frenchmen regard the Monte Carlo Rally as a native event. It was the brainchild of Antony Noghès, who in 1911 had the idea of a winter car rally starting from the capital cities of Europe and converging on Monte Carlo. At that time just to complete the course and arrive was a challenge in itself. The first event, which drew 23 entries, was won by Henri Rougier in a Turcat-Méry. It was repeated the following year but after that no rallies were held until 1925.

When it was revived the 'Monte' became a magnet for French manufacturers who quickly appreciated the publicity it attracted. Harsh weather frequently reduced the finishers

and it became a contest among highly efficient works teams. Much of the original appeal vanished in 1973 when the Monte became a round in the World Rally Championship. The separate starting points were abandoned. All competitors started from Monte Carlo and a series of special stages found the winner.

As well as devising the Monte Carlo Rally, the fertile mind of Antony Noghès also conceived the Monaco Grand Prix. From its first running in 1929 into the 21st Century the Grand Prix hugely surpassed the rally in the world of glamorous publicity.

go-kart. He became involved with the Winfield race-driving school at the Magny-Cours circuit and began building training cars for the school. When these were developed into Formula 3 machines, success soon followed. Jacques Laffite became French Formula 3 champion in 1973 with a Martini.

The next step was into Formula 2. In 1975 Martini used the almost universal BMW M12 engine, which took Laffite to the European Championship. The Renault CH1B engine was used in 1976 when René Arnoux was runner-up in a Martini. The 1977 season saw Arnoux as the European F2 Champion, still powered by Renault.

The 3.5-litre Hotchkiss 686 won the Monte Carlo Rally in 1939, 1949 and 1950.

Ambition being part and parcel of motor racing, in 1978 Tico Martini entered Formula 1 using the DFV Ford-Cosworth engine. Arnoux was the driver but the results were dismal and the F1 team disappeared at the end of the season. Martini went back to making F3 cars. Manufacture continued at Magny-Cours until 2000. The cars remained competitive, the last major result being the 1999 European F3 Championship, won by future F1 driver Sebastien Bourdais using an Opel engine.

GRAC, standing for Groupe de Recherche Automobiles de Course, was the Valence-based company of Serge Asiomanoff. He began building Formula France cars which were champions in 1968 and 1969. He moved on to F3 where results were unspectacular, so GRAC made another move in 1973 to cars for the European 2.0-litre Sports-Car Championship using Simca engines. After little success in two seasons, Asiomanoff gave up and in 1968 went back to engineering projects.

Amongst 'Les Autres' which carried French blue with varying degrees of success for over 100 years, the last word should go to Eugène Mauve. Mauve built a series of bizarre cyclecars constructed as tandem two-seaters. He seated the unfortunate passenger behind the driver and in front of an exposed engine. Mauve's machines raced in 1920 and 1921 with no success but compensated by provoking much mirth amongst onlookers. After Mauve gave up racing he took on the organisation of the successful Bol d'Or race series, which gave an outlet to many amateur constructors. Some had ideas almost as eccentric as those of Mauve himself.

Over the years countless enthusiastic constructors and drivers have sought glory in French-blue cars. Some showed great engineering ingenuity. Others might have achieved glory with a little luck or—more likely—with better finance. All enlivened the racing scene, inspired by a fervent desire to see the blue cars ahead of the rest.

The Martini MK23 made little impression on the F1 world in 1978.

Eugène Mauve competed in his bizarre Elfe cyclecar at Gaillon hill climb in 1920.

Bibliography

Ilu, Serge: *Blue Blood* (Frederick Warne 1979)
Blight, Anthony: *The French Sports Car Revolution* (G.T. Foulis 1996)
Boddy, William: *Montlhéry* (Cassel 1961)
Court, William: *Power and Glory* (McDonald 1966)
___ *Grand Prix Requiem* (Patrick Stephens 1992)
___ *The Racing Peugeots 1912-1919* (Profile Publications 1967)
Draper, Chris: *The Salmson Story* (David & Charles 1974)
Dreyfus, René (with Beverley Rae Kimes): *My Two Lives* (Aztex 1983)
Dumont, Pierre: *Peugeot* (E.P.A. 1976)
Georgano, Nick (Ed): *The Encyclopaedia of Motor Sport* (Ebury Press & Michael Joseph 1971)
___ *The Beaulieu Encyclopaedia of the Automobile* (The Stationery Office 2000)
Hodges, David: *The French Grand Prix* (Temple Press 1967)
Huet, Christian: *Gordini* (Editions Christian Huet 1984)
Jenkinson, Denis: *Motor Sport Racing Car Review* (Grenville 1947 & 1949)
Kupelian, Yvette and Sirtiane, Jacques: *Soixante Ans de Competition Automobile en Belgique 1896-1956* (Kupelian & Du Bock 2001)
Louche, Maurice: *Trintignant-Wimille* (Editions Maurice Louche 2003)
Mathieson, T.A.S.O.: *Grand Prix Racing 1906-1914* (Connaisseur Automobile 1965)
Moity, Christian, Teissedre, Jean-Marc and Bienvenue, Alain: *24 Heures du Mans 1923-1992* (Editions d'Art, J. P. Barthelemy 1992)
Nye, Douglas: *History of the Grand Prix Car 1945-65* (Hazelton 1993)
___ *History of the Grand Prix Car 1966-91* (Hazelton 1993)
Pacal, Domique with Francois Joly: *Les Grandes Heures de Montlhéry* (ETAI 2004)
Pomeroy, Laurence: *The Grand Prix Car* (Temple Press 1954)
Popely, Rick with L. Spencer Riggs: *Indianapolis 500 Chronicle* (Publications International 1998)
Posthumus, Cyril: *The 1906-1908 Grand Prix Renaults* (Profile Publications 1967)
___ *The 4½-litre Lago-Talbot* (Profile Publications 1973)
Rose, Gerald: *A Record of Motor Racing 1894-1908* (MRP 1949)
Sheldon, Paul: *A Record of Grand Prix and Voiturette Racing* Vols 1-13 (St Leonard's Press 1987-2002)
Small, Steven: *The Grand Prix Who's Who* (Guinness Publishing 1996)
Ulrich, Michael: *The Race Bugatti Missed* (Published by author 2005)
Venables, David: *Bugatti, A Racing History* (Haynes 2002)
Wimpffen, Janos L: *Time and Two Seats* (Motor Sports Research Group 1999)

Index